THE REBIRTH
OF LIBERAL EDUCATION

The Rebirth
of Liberal Education

BY

FRED B. MILLETT

HARCOURT, BRACE AND COMPANY · NEW YORK

A WARTIME BOOK

PRINTED IN THE UNITED STATES OF AMERICA

PREFACE

THIS study is based upon the assumption that liberal education is being or may be reborn wherever the humanities—literature, the arts, philosophy, religion, and history—are restored to the primary position in the college curriculum. The necessity for such a restoration resides in the fact that if the primary objective of liberal education is the analysis and discrimination of values, the humanities constitute the group of disciplines most vital to such analysis and discrimination. They are the disciplines most essential to such a purpose, because they, rather than the natural sciences or the social sciences, are concerned with values that may legitimately be called humane. Every group of disciplines has its particular and peculiar utility and value; the humanities transcend the other disciplines because of their concern, not with material or physical or social values but with intellectual, esthetic, moral, and spiritual values.

The major function of the liberal arts college should be the clarification and inculcation of the humanistic view of life. This view is not, to be sure, arrived at from an exclusive preoccupation with the humanities. In the modern world, humanism can hardly ignore such significant areas of human knowledge as the social and the natural sciences, but a genuinely liberal education will concern itself with these sciences not as techniques nor as preprofessional training but as areas concerned with a special variety of truth and with the development of appropriate methodologies. It must devote itself primarily to investigating the purposes

v

and methods and, more particularly, the philosophical assumptions of these subjects. Liberal education will never lose sight of the fact that any science becomes humanistic when it is approached not merely in its own peculiar terms but also philosophically and historically. Thus, any one of the natural or social sciences becomes a legitimate part of the humanistic curriculum when it is studied, not only scientifically but also historically and philosophically.

In the light of these convictions, I have, first of all, analyzed the reasons—historical and intellectual—for the loss by the humanities of their erstwhile primary position in higher education. These reasons I found to be the predominantly scientific and materialistic climate of the modern world, the competition offered the humanities by the multiplication of subject matters and departments, the consequent obscuration of the objectives of a genuinely liberal education, and the fact that the humanities, in order to defend themselves against their competitors, have attempted to become sciences themselves by applying inappropriate scientific methods to humanistic material.

I have then collected such evidence as time and opportunity permitted of attempts that are being made to revitalize and re-emphasize the humanities. These experimental attempts, I have found, take on the form of more or less extended educational programs designed to combat departmentalization in the area of the humanities or to give to the humanities the kind or degree of emphasis necessary for their restoration to a position of primacy in the college curriculum. Specifically, these experiments consist of single courses that link up the various departments in the humanities, or of a series of courses intended to furnish a common core of intellectual experience to all liberal arts students. A form of experimentation common to the humanities and to the other groups of intellectual disciplines is the devising of pedagogical techniques intended to eliminate the weaknesses of the conventional lecture-recitation-examination system. Such experimentation is variously apparent in tutorial or honors work, independent study, and the student-centered activities of some of the progressive colleges.

Since no system is superior to the human beings that operate it, I have attempted an informal survey of academic personnel in the field of the humanities and have suggested various means by which the quality of that personnel can be heightened.

Finally, I have indicated the major and minor problems that face liberal arts colleges intent on revitalizing their programs. In this connection, I have presented in some detail the reasons why I believe that in such programs the humanities must be restored to the position of primacy to which all other disciplines in the liberal arts college must be subordinated.

This study has grown out of an investigation I undertook at the request of David H. Stevens, Director of the Humanities Division of the Rockefeller Foundation. In the spring of 1942, he asked me to devote a period of eight months to visiting a number of colleges and universities where experimentation in the humanities was going on, and to write up my results. What he was most concerned with my observing was the nature and extent of programs in the humanities and the quality and training of the personnel in this field.

Accordingly, I visited the following institutions of higher learning: Reed, Scripps, Sarah Lawrence, Vassar, Bennington, and Hamilton Colleges, and Cornell, Michigan, Chicago, Iowa, California, Stanford, Colorado, Vanderbilt, Princeton, and Colgate Universities. In each college or university I visited, I held hourly interviews with fifteen or twenty members of the administration or of the specific humanities departments—language, literature, fine arts, music, philosophy, and history—and with a few members of other departments who were known for their interest in the problems I was investigating.

This account of my experience is to a considerable extent, therefore, devoted to an exposition of the aims of various programs and a description of the methods adopted for the attainment of these ends. The exposition and description of these experiments in program-building or in techniques of teaching are, I trust, accurately set forth. In most instances, they depend, not only on the official accounts of the programs and techniques but on the testimony of participants or my personal observation. The reader should, however, bear in mind the fact that the observations were made in 1942-1943, and that some of these programs have been curtailed as the war has made deeper and deeper inroads into the liberal arts colleges or have been modified—particularly in the case of the University of Chicago—in the light of earlier experience and of new ideas and objectives. The rest of the book—a consideration of the broader problems surrounding the humanities—is based, not only on the concrete experience of this investigation but also on thirty years of study and teaching in the field of the humanities. For the soundness or unsoundness of these more general observations, I am more than willing to assume complete responsibility.

The documentation is intended to parallel, to supplement, or to qualify the personal views expressed in the body of the text. To the writers of the numerous educational studies from which I have quoted, I should like to express my very sincere thanks.

My personal obligations are numerous but agreeable. Primarily, I am indebted to David H. Stevens not only for making it possible for me to secure a semester's leave of absence from Wesleyan University in order that I might give full time to this investigation, but also for advice and guidance and for an all-important initiation into the technique of interviewing of which he is an experienced master. I also want to express my appreciation of the courtesy and co-operativeness of the administrative officers of the institutions I visited and, particularly, of the efficient aid given me by their expert secretaries. I am obviously deeply indebted to the dozens of faculty members who gave me of their time and thought, even when they were not at all sure what I was after or what I was up to. Specifically, I should like to take this opportunity to suggest the pleasure I feel in remembering the cordiality of the hospitality offered me all along the way—a hospitality which, in the nature of the case, I was not in a position to repay.

F. B. M.

June 25, 1944
Wesleyan University
Middletown, Connecticut

CONTENTS

THE REBIRTH
OF LIBERAL EDUCATION

CHAPTER I

THE DECLINE OF THE HUMANITIES

THE growing literature on the nature, functions, and programs of the humanities is a significant index to the contemporary concern with the disciplines identified with this intellectual field. The breadth and depth of this concern may indicate that twentieth-century educators regard the humanities as of very great importance or that they consider that they are important but less vigorous than they should be. The presumption is that the humanities would not be the focus of such concentrated attention if they were in as flourishing a state as their adherents would desire. If the happy nation has no history and the healthy man is inappreciative of his condition until his health is threatened, we may assume that the attention given the humanities in the educational literature of the last generation indicates the conviction of many professional and amateur observers that the state of the humanities is unsound, that the humanities' lot, like Gilbert and Sullivan's policeman's, is not a happy one.

If this assumption is correct, the proper procedure perhaps is a diagnosis of the unhealthy state of the humanities. Such a diagnosis will, I believe, be most profitable if we attempt to distinguish between the environmental and the organic causes of this state. The environmental influences are the more obvious and may well be designated first.

The history of the curriculum of colleges and universities during the past century suggests one of the most objective of the environmental influences on the humanities. That history has been one of constant extension of the academic curriculum through the addition and inclusion of subjects distinct from the humanities and, in most instances, more or less alien to them. If one compares the curriculum of the small liberal arts college in 1840 with the curriculum of the same small liberal arts college in 1940, he is struck by the surprising increase in the number of subjects offered the twentieth-century undergraduate. A catalogue published in 1840 would probably show a curriculum limited to Greek and Latin, Mathematics, Philosophy, Natural Philosophy, and Rhetoric.* A similar catalogue published in 1940 shows a marked increase in subject matters: Art, Astronomy, Biology, Chemistry, Greek, Economics, English, French, Geology, German, Government, History, Italian, Mathematics, Latin, Music, Philosophy, Physical Education, Physics, Psychology, Religion, and Spanish.[1] Two developments are obvious from this juxtaposition. Natural Philosophy has divided and subdivided with the result that five important autonomous departments—Astronomy, Biology, Chemistry, Geology, and Physics—now compete for the student's attention and the administration's support. The social sciences—Economics and Government (or Political Science)—have established themselves in the academic stronghold. Psychology has broken away from its mother Philosophy, and is an uneasy stepchild of either the natural or the social sciences. This development, of course, is painfully familiar to students of the history of the academic curriculum; nevertheless, its familiarity should not dull the

* Carl F. Price's official history of Wesleyan University, *Wesleyan's first century* (Wesleyan University, 1932), reports that on the opening of this institution in 1831 its faculty was organized in five departments: Moral Science and Belles-Lettres, Mathematics, Ancient Languages and Literature, Natural Science, and Modern Languages (p. 43). By 1840, its departments were seven in number; Civil Engineering and Normal Instruction had been added to the original five (p. 64).

[1] Numbers refer to notes to be found at end of book.

4

edge of its significance. The traditional subjects—Greek, Latin, Mathematics, and Philosophy—have had to withstand the competition of an increasing number of other subject matters, young, ambitious, energetic, and sometimes self-important. This strenuous competition for gifted students and promising teachers has had the most fundamental effects on the state of mind and the morale of persons and institutions dedicated primarily to the humanities. Such persons have been driven to protect themselves by more or less devious means against a competition that in the smaller liberal arts institutions has been a struggle for "survival of the fittest," a struggle the brutality of which is obscured by the preservation of an appearance of toleration and good manners.

The situation of the humanities in the universities is even more hazardous than their position in the liberal arts colleges. For the American university in particular has tended to become a conglomeration of vocational and professional schools assembled incoherently around a nucleus of liberal arts education.[2] Medicine, law, theology, and business are the purely professional schools most frequently encountered in the privately endowed university. More insidiously, the American university—as distinguished from the English university, for example—has developed and magnified professional training, not only in the fields of the social and natural sciences, but in the humanities as well. The result is the imposition of graduate schools over and above the undergraduate liberal arts curriculum, with the natural growth of all sorts of impingements upon work on the undergraduate level and interference with it. Most impertinent of all has been the rise of professional training schools for secondary-school and high-school teachers, with their characteristic emphasis on methodology rather than on subject matter, on classroom procedures rather than on classroom performance.

In the state universities, the humanities are in still worse plight.[3] For the state universities feel compelled to offer not only all the types of training proffered by the endowed universities, but also types of training particularly pertinent to the political and economic unit on which the universities depend. Such training and such services, however admirable or however fantastic, are in large measure defensible on the ground that the university is a publicly supported institution and must serve its public intelligently or unintelligently. But, not content with the functions that might well be peculiar to themselves and might well justify their existence, the state universities not only have tended to do the work appropriate to their origin and situation, but have insisted on duplicating the development of graduate schools in the field of the pure sciences, the social sciences, and the humanities. One of the results of this duplication has been an overemphasis on the values of scholarship and research, the proliferation of scholarly magazines, and, with regard to the humanities, the further obscuration and distortion of the functions and procedures of the undergraduate liberal arts program.

The humanities have had to compete not only with the subject matters that have fought their way into the academic curriculum, but also with institutions founded primarily for the furtherance of a nonliberal (if not illiberal) education: the technical and vocational schools dedicated to the production of the applied scientists and the technicians, engineers, and mechanics demanded by a technological society. Such institutions offer the stiffest kind of intellectual competition to liberal arts colleges by drawing off endowments, pedagogical talents, and promising students that might otherwise have turned to institutions of the older liberal type.

The environmental influences thus far designated are matter of objective fact. Less objective but no less influen-

6

tial are the prevailing tone and temper of American life. Generalizations about the American spirit are dangerous, but there is overabundant evidence that the prevailing tone of American life is utilitarian and pragmatic. The normal extraverted American characteristically finds his values in things, not in ideas or attitudes, or in the possession of immaterial goods. Despite his good nature and his generosity, despite his ready response to human suffering, he finds the most defensible human goal in the successful life,[4] rather than the good life, and for him the most incontestable measure of success is the possession of things.[5] The psychological sources of this passion for success and this passion for things certainly lie very deep and are as certainly complex. Some of these sources are definitely historical: the frontier tradition and the pioneering spirit, the excessive mobility of American life, the absence of a rigid class system. Other sources are as certainly psychological: the conditioning of the individual into habits of extraversion through the absence of privacy in the typical American home and in the typical American public school and college and, perhaps even more significantly, the pressures of high-powered national advertising which itself is a by-product of our business and consumer economy.

The whole tone and temper of an industrial order in which the largest monetary rewards go to those who devote themselves to business enterprise have the most far-reaching effects upon the millions of aspirants for a success that can be measured in dollars and cents or in the material goods which dollars and cents can acquire. Operating under the impetus of the profit motive, business shrewdly gives its advertising the protective coloration of the service motive and thus builds up in the minds and imaginations of potential consumers the habit of identifying success in life with the accumulation of articles, mechanisms, and gadgets supposedly designed to increase physi-

7

cal comfort and to lend grace, elegance, and beauty to human lives. The humanities, then, conceiving of human values in the immaterial realm, find themselves struggling to make their voices heard in the babel borne in upon the reader and listener through all those media of communication that find their basic sustenance in high-powered advertising: the newspaper, the popular magazine, and the radio.

But perhaps the most dangerous foe of the humanities is one that dwells within and not without the academic citadel: science and the scientific method. In the intellectual history of the past century, nothing is more striking or portentous than the rise in prestige of the scientific spirit. The proliferation, division, and subdivision of the natural sciences; the vast extensions of knowledge resulting from a vigorous application of the scientific method to ever widening subject matters; the physical transformation of urban life through the union of science and technology—all these processes have made the profoundest impression on the minds of those engaged in humanistic studies. These inescapable impressions would have been legitimate and healthy if they had not caused to develop in the minds of the humanists a profound sense of inferiority which has led them to regard the humanities not as the crown and flower of liberal education—indeed the *sine qua non* of liberal education—but as perhaps the least defensible of intellectual preoccupations, a poor third in the hierarchy of values embodied in the physical sciences and the vigorous and challenging social sciences. There is perhaps a sense of inferiority that is rational; there is certainly a sense of inferiority that is irrational and neurotic, and the depression that has seized upon the minds of the humanists and undermined their morale has definitely neurotic characteristics.

Its neurotic character is apparent in the strategy the humanists adopted—if I may borrow a fruitful metaphor from

8

Kenneth Burke—by means of which they hoped to circumvent their demoralizing sense of inferiority. The rational and healthy way in which to circumvent their low state would have been the clarification of the differences between the humanistic and the scientific disciplines and the discrimination of the values peculiar to each of these major intellectual procedures. It would have been easy—and it is still easy—for the humanist to defend the values for which he stands by summoning arguments which on the face of them are in the nature of special pleading. The academic man is frequently a timorous animal, but, being human, he will, when cornered, use weapons with a considerable admixture of base alloys. If the classics and language study are defensible, they are defensible on grounds that any rational person would recognize as rational. If they are indefensible, no amount of special pleading will avail against the pressure of reality. Most of the arguments concerning the disciplinary value of this, that, or the other subject are equally and obviously specious.

But such a method of defense rapidly defeats itself. The humanists, however, were not satisfied with protecting their position by any argument on which they could lay hands. They undertook systematically to attack the enemy with his own weapons. If science was the order of the day, the humanists would turn themselves into scientists. The history of this transmogrification is one of the most painful chapters in the intellectual history of our time.

To the natural scientist, the attempt of the humanities to take over the scientific method and to apply it to the subject matters of such fields as language and literature, fine arts, music, philosophy, and history seems impracticable and inevitably unsuccessful. The natural scientist prides himself on dealing with objective data that are capable of careful manipulation and precise measurement. To such a man—in so far as he has any awareness of the values implicit in the humanities—the materials of the humanities seem so intangible and the values so subjective as to defy the successful application to them of the scientific method. But, despite the scientist's skepticism and his ill-concealed air of superiority, hundreds of workers in the humanities, at least since the nineteenth century, have trained themselves in the scientific method and have devoted themselves to applying it to humanistic subject matters.

The basic elements of the scientific method may perhaps be considered as the definition of a problem, the formulation of an hypothesis that promises a solution to the problem, the collection of evidence pertinent to the hypothesis, the objective weighing of the evidence, and the acceptance or rejection of the initial hypothesis in the light of the amassed evidence.[6]

From this statement it is obvious that the scientific method can be applied to some humanistic subject matters or to some aspects of some humanistic subject matters more successfully than to others. It is obvious, for example, that the success of the *historical* study of language and literature, fine arts, music, and philosophy will be proportionate to the fidelity and skill with which the scientific method is applied. In other words, in connection with humanistic studies, certain problems suggest themselves that can be solved only by the application of this method. Such problems are the appearance and diffusion of linguistic changes; the objective events in the lives of authors, artists, and philosophers; the appearance and development of technical tools in painting, sculpture, and music; the genealogical relationships of manuscripts; and the evolution of the manuscript in the hands of the author or in the printing and publishing house. Such problems, it should be observed, are those that rise in connection with man's curiosity concerning the facts relevant to the humanities, from his noble desire to eliminate ignorance and error, and to arrive at demonstrable truth.

There are, however, certain characteristics of humanistic material that complicate the successful application of the scientific method. One of these characteristics is the relative inaccessibility of the evidence, an inaccessibility that is not merely spatial but temporal. The evidence surviving from the past is likely to be not only fragmentary but inaccessible to the kind of control that the subject matters of chemistry and physics offer to scientific workers. Such evidence as has survived can be assembled, but it cannot be assembled with the ease or fullness offered by the materials with which the physicist, chemist, or biologist deals.* The temporal character of the evidence peculiar to humanistic studies raises another difficulty, the effect of time in refracting the vision of the scientific worker, and the consequent necessity for allowing for time's refraction. This difficulty, however, is only subsidiary to the major difficulty involved in applying the scientific method to humanistic material. This difficulty arises from the fact that in essence the humanistic studies—to a far greater degree than the natural sciences and the social sciences—involve problems of value. I. A. Richards has said, in a sentence pregnant with meaning, "The arts are our storehouse of recorded values." In this condition reside the special significance and importance of humanistic studies.

The problem that arises from this circumstance is whether or not the values peculiar to humanistic studies are capable of scientific treatment. Such values as are intrinsic in the physical sciences are available, one presumes, for scientific treatment. But such values are, in the nature

* Among the sciences, geology would seem to share some of the difficulties peculiar to the humanistic studies. Its primary concern is with the past, and its materials are incomplete and scattered and difficult to assemble and control.

of the case, objective and not subjective, whereas the values peculiar to humanistic studies are emphatically and inevitably subjective. The humanistic student, therefore, who limits his studies to those problems capable of solution by the application of the scientific method is confining his attention to the factual aspects of his subject matter and is neglecting or slighting the value-aspects.

History offers a conspicuous and incontestable illustration of the pertinence and the impertinence of the scientific method in humanistic studies. For a study of the factual aspects of history, the scientific method is fundamental and indispensable. The problem of whether Caesar did or did not cross the Rubicon, whether Charlotte Corday did or did not murder Marat in his tub, whether George Washington did or did not cut down a cherry tree are problems that the scientific method can go far toward solving. But whether Caesar did or did not cross the Rubicon would be a matter of complete insignificance—except to the remorseless antiquarian—if Caesar were not an important, problematical, and influential human being, and the problems of the nature and significance of historical personages are obviously problems of evaluation. When the historian deals—as he can hardly refrain from dealing unless he is content to be a barren chronicler of chaotic events—with the characters of historical personages, he can no longer remain objective. He must rely on intuition, understanding of human nature, tolerance, insight, and other powers of an intangible and subjective sort.[7] The great historian, then, will be a man who is not only faithful to the demands of the scientific method but skilled in the more difficult craft of interpretation and evaluation. He must be, in so far as his material permits, a scientist. He is forced by the nature of his material to be an artist also—that is, a man skilled in the discrimination, manipulation, and presentation of values.[8]

Among the humanistic disciplines, language is perhaps the one to which the scientific method is most appropriate. The evidence as to how ancient Greek or Old English was pronounced must remain imperfect and the conclusions problematical, but for the study of morphology, grammar, and semantics the scientific method is fundamental. Even here, however, it is worth noting that although it is possible for the linguistic historian to trace the development in the meanings of words, modern semantics—in the hands of such rivals as Richards and Korzybski—has demonstrated the tremendous part that affective coloration and emotional weighting play in modifying the meanings of words. It is enough to cite such a word as "communist" to illustrate the immense importance of the subjective elements and the affective aura in determining the meaning of a word. Probably the greater relevance of the scientific method to the study of language—as distinct from the study of literature —is due primarily to the differences and distinctions between language and literature. Language is obviously the medium; literature is what results from a skillful use of the medium. The one is means; the other is end.

This distinction throws light on the place of the scientific method in the study of the fine arts and music. In these fields, the scientific method is relevant and appropriate to the study of the factual aspects of the creative artists' lives; it is also relevant and appropriate to the study of the media peculiar to these arts. The physical processes involved in sculpture, painting, architecture, etching, and lithography are—like language—available for scientific study, as are the acoustical aspects of music and the evolution of musical instruments. But such studies, while important, quite fail to touch upon the value-aspects of works of art and must, at best, serve only as subsidiary contributions to the study of the value-aspects.

The pertinence of the scientific method to philosophy is

even less clear. The lives of philosophers and the history of their texts are obviously material for historical study, as indeed is the complex history of the relationship between one philosopher's system and another's. But, if philosophy is to have any higher function than the reconstruction of the intellectual history of mankind, it must concern itself with the validity of the philosophical systems studied; it must, in other words, concern itself, not merely with facts, not merely with ideas, but with the validity and value of the ideas.

Similarly the scientific method is appropriate to the study of certain aspects of literature, and completely inadequate to the study of other, and probably more important, aspects. The scientific method is appropriately applied to investigations concerning the lives of authors, the sources of their works, the process of evolution of a manuscript, and the history of their works in manuscript or print. But in the solution of more important problems of the nature and significance of their ideas, and the esthetic values of the specific works of art they have created, or the importance of the totality of their work, the scientific method is of absolutely no assistance.[9]

And yet, the training offered prospective teachers and scholars in the graduate schools of American public and private universities is almost solely training in the scientific method and in its application to one or another field of the humanities. The history of graduate study in the field of English literature may serve to illustrate the consequences of attempting to make the study of literature scientific. In the earlier stages of the evolution of the curriculum of graduate studies in English, it was assumed that no Doctor of Philosophy could be regarded as properly equipped for the teaching of Milton, Fielding, or Conrad unless he had a "sound" linguistic foundation of Gothic, Old and Middle English, Old and Medieval French, and possibly Old and

Middle High German. At that period, which lasted roughly up to the First World War, the only literary fields in English literature which were regarded as unequivocally respectable were Old and Middle English literature, and the literature of the Renaissance. At that time Milton was the most modern author to whom the methods of scholarship could be applied with impunity. The characteristic three-hour doctor's oral made a pretense of "covering" English literature from Beowulf to Thomas Hardy, but it bogged down in practice. Beginning with Beowulf, it dallied lovingly among the verbs of the third or fourth class in Old English and the major and minor dialects of Middle English and, if the student were wary, came to a glorious conclusion with the consideration of some fifth-rate dramatist of the English Renaissance.*

The arguments against extending the areas of scholarly study to include the eighteenth or nineteenth century were ingenious, if not persuasive. One of the most popular arguments against studying any literary figure later than Milton was the contention that for any figure later than Milton or any period later than the seventeenth century the materials were so overabundant that they were impervious to scientific treatment. One might have thought that the abundance of materials would have been an additional incentive to study rather than a deterrent. Another popular argument was the assertion that the nearer one came to modern literature, the more unstable were the critical judgments as to authors worth studying. The consequence of this argument in practice was that it was regarded as perfectly legitimate to study a tenth-rate medieval or Ren-

---

* The written comprehensive examinations now in vogue are a considerable improvement on the torture-rack of the doctor's oral, but, since the candidates have usually had no training in either esthetic or rhetorical analysis, the results are much more likely to show a wide reading in secondary sources than any fresh or penetrating personal reaction to the works set for examination.

15

aissance author but suspect to study a second-class figure in the nineteenth century. The study of twentieth-century literature was left to the mercies of unscholarly esthetes teaching courses for undergraduates who were naturally curious about the literature being produced by authors living in their own time.

Since the end of the First World War, the picture has changed slightly. Eighteenth-century literature has become the most respectable of all areas for graduate study, and the nineteenth century has arrived at least at the demimonde of scholarly society. Our own American literature—the one in which we should normally have the deepest interest—has attained a quasi-respectability, although a disproportionate amount of attention is still given to foreign literatures—English, French, German, Spanish, and Italian—in graduate courses and in scholarly publications.

But the gravest error of the American graduate schools was the focusing on an approach to literature—legitimate, to be sure, for certain purposes—to the exclusion of training in other approaches to literature more appropriate and more basic to an illumination of the subject matter. The calm assumption of the designers of the graduate curriculum was that if students were trained in techniques for establishing the facts about literature, they could be left safely to establish the values of literature for themselves. As anyone who has had any experience in teaching graduate students will testify, such an assumption could be entertained only by a prolonged devotion to the technique of the ostrich in avoiding an enemy. With taste, with critical or esthetic principles, with even the ability to read a single text intelligently, the average graduate student is pathetically unequipped. And yet, despite the esthetic and intellectual poverty of the average graduate student, the current conventional graduate program in English studies offers no training in taste and no systematic training in critical principles or theoretical or applied criticism. In no graduate course, within the range of my own experience, was there ever raised any question of taste, or of the esthetic or philosophical values in any of the works of art allegedly under scrutiny.[10]

A similar procedure applied to the study of the fine arts has had the most distressing consequences. One would have thought that the primary problems raised by a painting are those of the interpretation and evaluation of the qualities it has as an art-form expressing something the artist regarded as worth painting. Instead, graduate training in art has very largely been, not training in the methods of interpretation and evaluation, but a study of the techniques and mechanics of works of art, a study of the means instead of a study of the end. In consequence, it is commonly considered more important for a graduate student to be equipped with vast stores of facts about the location of works of art or about their technical aspects than for him to be equipped with a method for evaluating the works of art whose technique he has studied. Thus, it is commonly regarded as more important to be able to identify a painting as showing the brush-work characteristic of a painter's third period than it is to be able to defend rationally a judgment that a particular work of art belongs to the third rank among an artist's work.

I have no desire to underestimate the value or the importance of training in the scientific method as applied to the humanities. What I am contending is that the typical American graduate school has given training in this method a prominence far beyond its deserts and has neglected shamefully other types of training more appropriate to the humanities. The results of this exclusive preoccupation with the scientific method have been unfortunate for scholarship itself, for the men trained to be scholars, and for the undergraduates who have suffered from their ministrations.

17

One of the serious results of the primacy of the scientific approach to humanistic studies has been its influence in breaking up the subject matter of the field into smaller and smaller segments, with the resulting departmentalization and compartmentalization of knowledge.[11] This process of departmentalization is regrettable for many reasons. One is the encouragement of a kind of academic nearsightedness, the inability to see the intellectual forest for the trees. Another consequence of this process of division and sub-division is that the advanced student is encouraged to specialize in a very small area of some one humanistic study. Thus, each incipient scholar is persuaded to become a specialist in Old French or the sixteenth-century Flemish painters or the music of Palestrina, and henceforth, if he remains faithful to his vows, he will be known in academic circles by his "subject," as though it had been stamped indelibly upon his soul. Neither he nor his students after him are encouraged to relate his subject to the rest of his field, and he would certainly be deemed heretical and damnable if he attempted to relate his subject to another field than his own, if he attempted, for example, to relate the sumptuous eroticism of Marlowe's *Hero and Leander* with the lush treatment of classical subject matters by the painters of the Italian Renaissance. A further evil—especially unfortunate in the small college—is the development of departments into autonomies with vested interests that they attempt to preserve in the strenuous competition for raises in salary and promotions.[12] Intellectually, the results have been even more disastrous, since each department develops the habit of thinking of its own subject as the all-important one, and one that must be preserved from contamination by any other subject and from any process of infiltration.[13] Most liberal arts colleges, therefore, are leagues of more or less amicable sovereign states,

18

each of which is intent on preserving its own sovereignty unsullied and unimpaired. The only issue on which the league itself is inclined to act co-operatively is the opposition to presidents or trustees proposing measures that threaten their separate or corporate sovereignties.

Humanistic scholarship is a production of the scientific method, or it is not, in the accepted sense of the word, scholarship. Quantitatively, the scholarly productions of Americans, since the appearance in our educational system of the full-fledged graduate school, have been almost overwhelmingly impressive. Qualitatively, the results are more questionable. For it is not merely pertinent but necessary to raise the question of value with regard to scholarship as with regard to the literature of which scholarship should be the humble handmaiden. In methodology and scholarly technique—the basic but still minor values of scholarship— American scholarship rates high, perhaps because methodology and technique are easy to teach, particularly to Americans who seem to have a decided gift for them. In brilliance of hypothesis and intellectual scope and ratiocinative subtlety, American scholarship makes a far less distinguished showing.

The production of Ph.D. theses has become the major concern and preoccupation of the graduate school, and it is not surprising, in a country dedicated to doing things in a big way—whether it is building dams or making bathtubs—that the quantity of Ph.D. theses far outdistances that of the German universities in the utterly demoralized period after the First World War.* Every dissertation—in

* The decline in quality of the German Ph.D. thesis is notorious. The time has long since passed when a German Ph.D. degree, whether held by a national or a foreigner, has had any intellectual standing or rating. One of the grimmest of academic sights is the collection of trifling and insignificant German Ph.D. theses awaiting cataloguing in an American university library. The librarian's curious code requires their cataloguing even at a cost far in excess of their worth. In the decline and fall of the German Ph.D. thesis, there is a warning for all of us.

most graduate schools, even the master's dissertation—is supposed to be and sometimes on its publication is attested to be "a contribution to scholarship," but whether the contribution is more than the widow's mite is another and more important question. Who is so inexperienced as not to recognize the stigmata of the ordinary Ph.D. thesis: an industrious accumulation of facts more or less relevant to a subject of supreme unimportance; the conscientiously constructed "scholarly" apparatus of footnotes, bibliography, and acknowledgments; the dedication to the fond wife or mother without whose assistance and encouragement the wretched product would never have seen the light of day; a painstakingly dull and pedestrian style; and a great air of arriving—like the mountain bringing forth the mouse—at a conclusion of obviously trivial significance.[14] In eight cases out of ten, moreover, the process of producing this *chef-d'œuvre* proves so exhausting to its creator that he never brings himself to the creation of any further scholarly work, although in the interests of academic advancement he may dissever his masterpiece and present its fragments to the world in the form of scholarly articles. By that time the scholarly vein is exhausted, and the producer lapses into the happy unproductivity of an assistant professorship in a college of agriculture.

The only circumstance that prevents the Ph.D. thesis' becoming a national scandal is the fact that most universities have the good sense not to publish the productions of their victims *in toto*. Instead, as a face-saving device, there has developed the habit of publishing summaries of theses —a device that is perhaps as harmless as any that can be devised short of complete suppression. It would probably be agreed among American scholars that those universities that persist in requiring the publication of their students' theses detract from their own reputations by so doing, since they thus unashamedly bare their own shortcomings to the scholarly world's scrutiny.*

The prolonged primacy of the scientific approach to literature and the training and productivity that have resulted from this primacy are less serious bibliographically than the results of this training and productivity on a majority of the men who attain the Ph.D. degree. Generalization as to the primal quality of the men who go in for the Ph.D. in the humanities would be dangerous and completely "unscientific." I doubt, however, whether the young men who go out from the colleges and who enter one or another of the humanistic departments are any less vital than those who choose the departments of chemistry or political science. Possibly they are, as a group, somewhat more sensitive, a little more impractical, although they are certainly not more introverted than the typical physical scientist. What is shocking is what the graduate school does to the human material with which it works. On the whole, I should be willing to defend the proposition that most of the men who complete their work for the Ph.D. degree are less vital, less broad-minded, less humane, more narrow in interests than they were when they entered the graduate school. Anyone who has observed the passage of students through the graduate school will have noticed how fre-

* Someone would do the academic world a service if he were to attempt to list the major contributions to American scholarship in the twentieth century. The publication of such a list would probably end in the assassination of the editor, but the service he had rendered would more than compensate for his demise. By way of illustration of what I mean by major contributions to American scholarship, I shall take the risk of giving two or three examples: John Livingston Lowes's *The road to Xanadu*, George Sherburn's *The early career of Alexander Pope*, and Newman I. White's *Shelley*. V. L. Parrington's *Main currents in American thought*, one of the most influential books of our time, would certainly not be regarded as a "scholarly" work by most of the academic *genus*. There have been of course some admirable editorial performances—such as the Columbia *Milton* and Hebel's *Drayton*—but such productions, though useful, are not exactly creative.

quently there takes place a slow drying up of the personality and its movement in the direction of narrowness and pedantry.

The effects of the scientific method on humanistic studies in the graduate school and its effect on the victims of that academic torture-house are less serious than the effects upon undergraduate education in the field of the humanities. For the objective of the training in the American graduate school is allegedly preparation for the teaching of undergraduate students. It is problematical whether any graduate training could be devised that is less calculated to produce the kind of teachers humanistic studies demand at the undergraduate level.[15] These studies call for teachers with vitality, with broad esthetic and cultural interests, with sharpened critical faculties, with far-ranging intellectual curiosity. Graduate education in the humanities is much more likely to send out into undergraduate teaching men with low vitality, narrow interests, naive esthetic and critical judgments, and an intellectual curiosity that is either nonexistent or is limited to a very narrow corner of the field the teacher has been tilling. The results on the undergraduates that are submitted to the instruction of such men can easily be imagined. Only students who have a very vigorous interest in the humanities or those who think that, at any rate, the humanities will be less intellectually arduous than the physical sciences or even the social sciences are likely to elect to major in one of the subjects in this field. It is at the level of undergraduate education that the process of liberal education should be at its most vital, should attain its most far-reaching results. That such is not the case is apparent in the widespread dissatisfaction with the achievement of the humanities in the liberal arts college. If there were not an abundance of evidence that this dissatisfaction were taking a practical and dynamic form, the prospects for the humanities would look dark indeed.

22

CHAPTER II

EXPERIMENTAL PROGRAMS AND COURSES

THE widespread feeling that the humanities have been in a slow state of decline and have been gradually losing their vitality has brought about, during the last decade and a half, the creation of a variety of programs and courses intended to eliminate some of the weaknesses of the conventional humanities programs in liberal arts colleges and universities.[1] In the main, the primary objective of these new programs and courses seems to be the combating of the deep-seated tendency toward departmentalization exhibited by the humanities during the latter part of the last century.[2] It is the purpose of this chapter to describe certain of these new programs and courses that have attracted attention and provoked discussion. Inevitably, many interesting experiments must be ignored in a study limited in length,[3] but the examples discussed have been chosen with a view to suggesting the variety of structure and devices intended to combat the tendency toward departmentalization.[4]

First to be considered are those single courses that cut across departmental lines; secondly, programs intended to encourage interdepartmental relationships; and, finally, programs that have the purpose of furnishing liberal arts students a common intellectual experience.

The number of courses that cross departmental boundaries is now almost legion. Historically, they seem to have been devised and worked out first in the field of the social sciences. Thereafter, the patterns and techniques were extended to include two or more of the humanistic disciplines. Such courses are now so numerous that we can do no more than cite a number of examples in this connection.*

One of the most common of the interdepartmental courses is that in the History of Civilization, of which Stanford University furnishes a convenient example. The course runs throughout the academic year, and the texts used are E. M. Burns's *Western civilizations, their history and their culture* and J. H. Randall's *The making of the modern mind.* There is a good deal of supplementary reading in the primary sources and the literature of the periods covered and constant stress on the works of art of these periods. The first third of the course sketches in man's cultural history from 3000 B.C. to 800 A.D.; the second third of the course brings the student through the period of the French Revolution; the final third of the course concludes with the events leading up to the outbreak of the Second World War. Although the chronological range of the course is overpowering, the emphasis is not narrowly historical but broadly cultural as may be seen from the subjects of lectures from one or another portion of the course: the emergence of Hebrew monotheism, Greek drama, the art of war in the ancient world, Mohammed and the rise of Islam, medieval towns, St. Thomas Aquinas, Puritanism

* Analogous to the courses with which we are concerned here are the orientation courses offered to freshmen with the purpose of facilitating their adjustment from a domestic to an academic environment and sometimes stressing the social and sometimes the intellectual aspects of the process. Related to the freshman orientation courses is such a course as the so-called Campus Course at the University of Iowa, initiated by a brilliant teacher and dramatic classroom lecturer, with the intention of providing students with a wide range and variety of stimulating intellectual experiences. Such a course, to be sure, is unique and inimitable, but its great success seems due, not only to the brilliance of the teacher but to the perhaps unconscious appetite of the students for a broadly oriented introduction to the intellecual life of the University.

24

as a cultural influence in Europe and America, nineteenth-century music, Stalin and the Soviet State. A new course in American Civilization recently launched at Stanford furnishes another illustration of the broader conceptions of history that now make for a richer synthesis of humanistic elements. A sufficient indication perhaps of the nature of this attempt to integrate various cultural phenomena in a revealing and suggestive pattern is furnished by such lecture subjects as the American land, economic and social transplantation from England to America, painting in provincial America, the enlightenment in the American colonies. These topics, chosen from the first third of a course that covers the first two centuries of America's history, indicate something of the emphases and proportions of this interdepartmental venture.

A more audacious utilization of interdepartmental courses is made at Bennington College where all the so-called Basic Courses, which are to be taken during the first two years of the student's career, are planned and worked out on nondepartmental lines. As examples of such courses, I may mention the following: Concepts and Methods of Social Science, The Nature of Physical Science, The Western Tradition in Literature and Philosophy, Non-rational Expression of Human Nature. The official descriptions of two of these courses suggest their points of view and procedures. The aims and contents of the course in the Concepts and Methods of Social Science are thus set forth:

The aim is to study social science as an important type of human behavior and a major influence in the modern world, rather than as a body of specific subject matter or the techniques of a particular field. The social significance of science, including its relation to human values, is the main point of reference. The first topics dealt with are: the culture as a surviving residue of past and present social behavior and its products: the patterns of culture, that is, the language, folkways,

25

conventions, traditions, customs, mores and institutions common to all human social groups, individual behavior as segments of these patterns, and these patterns as activities constituting the values desired by the group. The second large area is a study of the scientific pattern of behavior, including technology as a principal aspect of contemporary culture; the assumptions, the logic, and the methods of science; their history, growth, present status, and future prospects; and finally, a consideration of selected aspects of contemporary culture from the scientific point of view.*

The aim of the course in The Western Tradition in Literature and Philosophy is identical with that of the course in Literature and the Humanities, that is, to help the student to make an adequate response to some of the more important forms of verbal expression that have emerged in Western culture. Emphasis is on training the intelligence and sensibility through discussion and intensive analysis of a few selected texts. In the course in The Western Tradition, the materials represent "most of the major literary forms as well as . . . the more important historical epochs . . ."

The Judeo-Christian influences will be studied in selections from the *Old* and the *New Testament;* the Mediaeval period in selections from *The Canterbury Tales* of Chaucer; the tradition of Greek Humanism in the *Oedipus Rex* of Sophocles; and the Renaissance and the beginnings of the modern world in readings from Erasmus, Pico, Montaigne, Bacon, Descartes and others having as their center the *Anniversaries* of John Donne.†

In addition to courses of which the purpose is the breaking down of departmental lines and the building up of significant relationships among the subjects within a broad

* "Announcement for the Year 1942-43," *Bennington College Bulletin,* Vol. X, No. 4, p. 21.
† *Ibid.,* p. 23. For some account of the courses in Literature and the Humanities, The Language of Music, and Analysis of Visual Art, see Chapter IV of this survey.

area of knowledge, there is an increasing number of programs that further these same objectives but cover more than a single year of the student's course. We shall turn now to a consideration of a number of programs that illustrate this type of educational experiment.

We may well take as our first example of this type of program the Divisional Humanities Program at Princeton, since it has been in operation for a number of years and since its principles and practices have been rather fully set forth by the members of the faculty who have participated in shaping them. The Divisional Program in the Humanities grew out of a realization that Princeton students were unaware of the wider implications of their departmental work. Some of the members of the faculty also felt that the students were "cashing in" on the benefits of their specialization only at the end of their senior year, and that some scheme should be devised to get these results earlier in the students' course. A committee was formed to devise a suitable program "to restore the grounds of understanding which make co-operation in the humanities a fruitful enterprise," to make the students aware of the wider implications of their departmental work, and to reap the benefits of the students' specialization. This committee consisted of a representative of each of six departments of the humanities: Arts, Classics, English, History, Modern Languages, and Philosophy. This committee worked out a program that makes it possible for a student to complete his departmental specialization in his second and third years, take his comprehensive examination at the end of his junior year, and devote his senior year to the task of integrating his departmental work with work in other departments in the humanities.

According to this plan, each student by the end of his sophomore year has taken at least two year-courses in one of the six humanistic departments, one year-course in each

27

of the other four humanistic departments, and one year-course in the natural sciences. The two year-courses in one of the humanistic departments constitute the beginning of his departmental specialization. In addition to advising the freshman as to what courses he should take to lay proper foundations for his divisional work in the humanities, the committee also offers a short sophomore course in Evidence and Interpretation. The student continues through his junior year to elect two year-courses in his department. During his junior year, the student works primarily as a departmental student, and he completes this work by the comprehensive examination he takes at the end of that year. During his senior year, the student works under the divisional committee as a whole, has various conferences with the committee alone, and meets occasionally with the committee and all the other seniors working under this program. His thesis-subject has been approved by the end of his junior year, and he is expected to read around his subject during the vacation between his junior and senior years. During his senior year, he takes three courses in the humanities departments that are relevant to his thesis. During the second semester of his senior year, the student is free from course requirements. The thesis-subject is very carefully chosen, and involves at least three departments in the humanities group. The topic is one that can be treated organically and not merely additively. The committee envisages three essential steps in its program: the laying of the foundation; specialization in a department; synthesis of the departmental work with the humanities generally. It also distinguishes three approaches to the subject matter of the humanities: chronological; systematic; and esthetic-critical, and it has attempted to give proper attention to each of these approaches in their training of students.

The members of the committee believe that their program has the following distinctive features:

(1) The members of the committee "have, over a period of years, made progress in mastering the difficult technique of achieving a common language and a common understanding of basic issues."

(2) "Each student in the Program has the benefit of individual interviews with members of the committee throughout his college course . . . This individual guidance is supplemented by the regular conferences designed to meet the developing interests and needs of the students."

(3) "The Program seeks to combine the advantages of specialization and wider orientation . . . It emphasizes the value of acquiring special competence in one field by learning, so far as an undergraduate can do so, what it means to master a given subject matter. But it also helps the student to study this subject in its relation to other subjects and thus to discover for himself that most problems of human significance cut across departmental boundaries."

(4) "The Program helps the student to become more literate and articulate, to respect accurate factual information, and to understand more fully the basic values of art, morality, and religion by studying with imaginative and critical sensitivity the great historical achievements in these realms."

(5) "The Program also stimulates the teaching powers of the faculty, since those who participate in it are inevitably called upon to make certain that the minds and the abilities of their students are developing continuously and in very concrete ways." *

The program of the newly organized School of Humanities at Stanford University is at an early stage of operation, but some notion of its objectives can be gleaned from the description of it by Lewis Mumford, who in 1942 was appointed Professor of Humanities in the School. The

---

* Quoted from a statement of the Committee of the Divisional Program of the Humanities.

program of the School of Humanities can be stated in fairly simple terms. The undergraduate prepares for his work in the School by taking a required course in the History of Western Civilization in his freshman year, and a course in the History of American Civilization in his sophomore year. Both these courses—of which the second has been recently designed and organized—stress the cultural aspects of history rather than the political and dynastic elements. During the student's junior and senior years, he works directly under the auspices of the School of Humanities. In his junior year, he will take a required course in the humanities. "This," according to Professor Mumford, "will involve a fundamental study of man conceived as a being trying to understand, to adapt himself to, and to adapt to himself, the natural environment in which he is placed, the social environment created by the fact of fellowship, and the realm of 'value' which he discovers both within and outside himself. Despite its scope, it will not be a survey course, but on the contrary will endeavor to treat its problems by intensive study and discussion, both in lectures and in small conference groups, of very specific cases and situations involving such questions." In his senior year, the student will take course-work appropriate to his interests, will supplement these courses with independent study, and will attend an all-year seminar related to his major interests. "In this seminar he will prepare a special study which will not merely represent very thorough research on a limited topic, but likewise assist the student to correlate all his humanistic studies and to grasp their meaning not as glittering generalities but rather as the core of concrete and vivid experience." *

It would be unfair, of course, to compare a program at its initial stage with such a program as that of the Divis-

* The School of Humanities, a description (Stanford University, California, n.d.), pp. 11-12.

30

ional Humanities at Princeton that has been in operation over a period of years. It is obvious, however, that at this stage the Stanford program is not so carefully integrated throughout the student's course as is the Princeton program, and that it does not provide clearly for the balance between specialization and nonspecialization that the Princeton program provides. Experience will probably show the desirability of providing a sharper focus for the student's program through his concentrating on a departmental program, while relating it to its divisional orientation.

Another type of anti-departmental program is that built, not on divisional lines but on two related subject matters. Such a type of program may be illustrated from the American Civilization program now operative at Princeton. Professor Willard Thorp has stated the objectives of this program thus: It is the aim of the program to lead students

to an understanding of our civilization as a living culture with established traditions and to an appreciation of its significance among other world civilizations. This understanding can be achieved only if the subject is approached from as many directions as possible; hence the necessity for combining within the program studies in both the social sciences and the humanities . . .

Briefly, the scheme of organization is as follows. A student enters the program at the time when he is admitted to one of the six departments which co-operate in its administration. He follows the regular program of study of his department, concentrating on the American aspects of his discipline to the extent the department prescribes. Under the supervision of his department's representative on the committee (who is also his departmental supervisor), the student writes his thesis—on an American subject. It is also required that he shall take during his last two years at least two courses in the American field. These courses must represent, severally, the following approaches to the subject: historical, institutional, philosophical, literary or artistic. As a senior the student participates in the sessions of a conference which investigates as comprehensively as possible some problem of fundamental importance in our culture.*

Such a program, obviously, is an attempt to integrate the student's experience in the various disciplines through focusing his study on American civilization in its various aspects.

It is noteworthy that both this program and the Princeton and the Stanford Divisional Humanities programs are under the control of committees made up of men from the various disciplines involved. The substitution of committee-control of programs for departmental control—an organizational device clearly intended to combat bad departmental habits—may be illustrated further by a number of committees set up in recent years at the University of Chicago. These committees offer—at least in print—much less detailed descriptions of their programs, and it would seem that their appeal is to a rather special type of student whose interests are broader than those of most departmental programs. The Princeton and Stanford Humanities programs and the Princeton American Civilization program have the very distinct advantage of clear statements as to the requirements for undergraduates embarking on such programs and of programs so conceived that they are likely to draw in other undergraduates than those already characterized by broad interests.

The Division of the Humanities at Chicago includes two such committees, one on Literature, and the other on the History of Culture. The Committee on Literature makes the following statement of its objectives and methods:

* "The Program of Study in American Civilization," *Princeton Alumni Weekly*, September 4, 1942, pp. 4-5. Somewhat similar programs had already been initiated at Harvard, Pennsylvania, Yale, Smith, and Williams. Professor Thorp regards the Williams program as closest to that at Princeton.

Students in the Division of the Humanities primarily interested in literature may have the opportunity of pursuing programs of study and research for the various degrees in fields which involve a combination of two or more national literatures. . . . Studies in literature may be oriented in two directions: (1) toward the theory of literature as a fine art and the application of theory to particular literary works (i.e., literary criticism); and (2) toward the historical study of literary productions and taste.*

The Committee on the History of Culture states its objectives thus:

A student working under the direction of this Committee selects as his field of concentration a particular period or domain of culture, and he is expected to study the political and social history, the literature, art, science, philosophy, and religion that appertain to the field selected. The Committee may accept as a field of concentration any well-recognized subdivision of culture history which it considers sufficiently comprehensive for the purpose and in which the requisite courses of instruction are available. Most students select one of the following fields: 1, Ancient oriental culture; 2, Classical culture; 3, Medieval culture; 4, Renaissance culture; 5, Modern European culture; 6, American culture; 7, Modern Oriental culture.†

Another principle of interdepartmental organization, and one that includes disciplines from several or all of the basic fields of knowledge, is the principle of national or regional culture. Programs to which the name of "Regional Majors" was given were initiated in the autumn of 1942 in the College of Arts and Sciences of the University of California under the guidance of Dean Joel E. Hildebrand. Dean Hil-

* "The Summer Quarter, 1942," *The University of Chicago: Announcements for sessions of 1942-43,* p. 65.

† *Ibid.,* p. 66. Both these committees work almost exclusively with candidates for the master's or the doctor's degrees, but since the principle of organization and the objectives resemble the programs already described, there seems sufficient reason for including them here.

debrand feels that Regional Majors can be justified on at least two significant grounds: first, the need of graduates broadly trained in all the relevant knowledge concerning countries in South America or in Europe; and second, the need for vitalizing the study of the linguistic, literary, and artistic aspects of a culture by placing them in the matrix of the total cultural, geographical, and racial situation of the country. Dean Hildebrand feels that a considerable number of Regional Majors can be launched immediately, at least in a state university having on its staff a large number of specialists in some aspect of an important cultural Region. This program is to be offered to undergraduate students who, it is hoped, will find in it a significant principle for integrating their studies. It should furnish a much better foundation for graduate work—at least in the field of social sciences and the humanities—than the conventional major built around a single subject, such as English or economics.

A final manifestation of the desire to build undergraduate education on other than departmental lines may be seen in the Honors program developed at the University of Michigan. The objective of the program for Honors work in Liberal Arts is the training of the student in a broader intellectual experience than that furnished by the Departmental Honors programs. In most instances, the tutors attempt to build up relationships, not only within an intellectual area but between one major intellectual area and another. Under this plan, the student is admitted to the Liberal Arts Honors program at the end of his sophomore year on the basis of his academic record, a personal interview with the Board of Tutors, and a qualifying examination that consists of tests of the student's knowledge of one foreign language, and of his ability to read and interpret a piece of imaginative writing and a piece of expository writing. In terms of courses, the only prerequisites for Honors work are Freshman English and a course in the History of Civilization. During the student's junior and senior year, he takes, along with a certain number of regular courses, an Honors seminar which is conducted by one of the members of the Board of Tutors. The student "is permitted to follow his special interest within the limits of the field of study of his particular group. The tutor in charge of the group has freedom to plan a program which is peculiarly suited to the needs of the individual student and one which will bring forth his best efforts . . . In the senior year each student is expected to write an essay upon a subject selected by him in consultation with his tutor." * Whether or not he is awarded Honors depends on the quality of the senior essay and the student's standing in his concentration examination and in the general examination given to all Honors students. What differentiates this Honors system from that of most institutions is its avowed purpose of breaking down departmental lines and of training the student in making significant connections between the subject in which he is specializing and some other subject in another basic area of knowledge. The members of the faculty who make up the Board of Tutors are all men who are interested in giving their students a type of training that shall be not only intensive but extensive. Though each tutor is free to plan his program for his tutorial group, the programs are aimed at achieving, in their very diverse ways, the common objectives of the Liberal Arts Honors program.[5]

The motivation of the programs intended to furnish liberal arts students a common intellectual experience is clear. It is the feeling that the elective system has resulted in what has been called education in the cafeteria style, an

* "College of Literature, Science, and the Arts, Announcement, 1941-42," *University of Michigan Official Publication* (1941), Vol. 34, No. 24, pp. 177-78.

education that is frequently planless, and that is all too often determined by the individual student's superficial interests and aptitudes, and his desire to enjoy as painless as possible an educational experience. The first stage of the reaction against education in the cafeteria style was the system of distribution and concentration now a familiar feature of the curriculum of the conventional liberal arts college.[6] The intention of this system was to secure each student's contact with the major fields of knowledge, usually the humanities, the social sciences, and the natural sciences. This system was obviously a step in the right direction, but it was only a halfhearted effort to provide the student with a satisfactory orientation in the basic elements in modern culture. It did not ensure the student's understanding the significance of the scattered courses chosen in the basic fields, nor did it ensure his seeing the relevance of one field to another or getting an over-view of the whole complex of modern culture. Moreover, it provided liberal arts students with little or no common intellectual ground, or sense of intellectual or cultural solidarity with their fellows, or even with the elements of a vocabulary of communication in the various fields of knowledge. To circumvent the shortcomings of the distribution-and-concentration system, a number of programs have been devised of which the overt intention is, not only orienting the student in the basic fields of knowledge but also furnishing him with a considerable amount of intellectual experience shared explicitly with his fellows.

Of the programs in this category, the so-called Colgate Plan was one of the first to be initiated and is one that has attracted very wide attention and induced frequent imitation. The assumptions that underlie the courses at Colgate that furnish students a common intellectual experience are thus stated by Professor E. G. Bewkes:

There is a felt need for knowledge about the physical and social world about us. Even the primitive man satisfied this need. The content of knowledge changes with the experience of the race, but the need for knowledge values remains. And, in like manner, there are other categories into which we classify our basic experiences, such as esthetic, moral, and religious, and these represent fundamental outlets of our human nature. It is in the actuality of living out these fundamental drives or urges that the human species finds its satisfactions— satisfactions in the doing as well as in the creative end results of action. It is just here that the worths or values of life are discernible, and it is also just here that the clue to a purposeful educational theory can be discovered.*

In order that each student may come into contact with the subject matter and the methodology of each of the fields of human experience in which these basic drives operate, Colgate University requires each student to take a series of five survey courses in (1) Philosophy and Religion, (2) Social Science, (3) Biological Science, (4) Physical Science, and (5) Fine Arts and Literature.[7] Each course runs through a single semester, and for each of these courses, except the last, the Colgate faculty has produced texts that are in use in a considerable number of other institutions.[8] The survey classes meet four times a week in small groups of not more than eighteen to a class. Normally, a student takes two of the survey courses in each semester of his freshman year and the fifth—the Survey of Fine Arts and Literature—during his sophomore year.

Of the conception of the survey course implicit in the Colgate system, Professor Bewkes writes:

The survey courses taken together represent the minimum or broad base of general education. . . . Any survey course as such must provide two things: first, it must, as the term im-

* E. G. Bewkes, "The Colgate Plan," in *General education* (1934), Vol. VI, p. 108.

plies, actually survey a broad field or closely related fields of human knowledge and interests; second, it must be so arranged that it will contain much definite knowledge content, creating genuine appreciation of the character and nature of the field studied. . . . A survey course must stand out as a unified whole bringing into view and use fundamental concepts and contributions of the various subjects included in a field.*

Aside from the values these courses have in introducing these students systematically to the basic fields of knowledge and initiating all students into the same educational experience, there are other arguments for making them the central core of an undergraduate's program.

There is a psychological factor brought into being by the survey courses which is a valuable educational asset. They do make the first year of college really something novel and fresh. Instead of college being just more of the same kind of thing the students have had in preparatory school, they are now introduced to the fields of knowledge from a different point of view and in a new way. There is a better appreciation of the interrelatedness and significance of the content and nature of the academic pursuits. There is created, in consequence, a zest which is often otherwise absent.†

The early stages (1931-38) of the Chicago College Plan, a program even more widely known and discussed than the Colgate Plan, showed significant resemblances to it, and differences from it. Like the Colgate Plan, the objective of the Chicago College Plan was the introduction of all undergraduate students to the basic fields of knowledge.‡ This

* Bewkes, *op. cit.,* pp. 111-12.
† *Ibid.,* p. 112.
‡ Since the survey courses given during the earlier stages of the Chicago College Plan are more nearly comparable to the other survey courses considered here, those earlier courses are the ones described and evaluated here. The reader who is interested in following the evolution of the survey courses in the curriculum of the new "four-year" College at Chicago is urged to consult *The University of Chicago An-*

objective, as officially stated, was "the attainment of the minimum essentials of factual information and an introduction to the methods of thought and work in each of four fields—the biological sciences, the humanities, the physical sciences, the social sciences—such as may be expected of a student who has pursued through an academic year a general course at the junior college level in each of the four fields." * The University, therefore, provided a one-year course in each of these four fields as a means of assisting the student in the attainment of the objective stated above. "The Introductory General Courses are presented by the lecture method, supplemented by small group discussions and by individual conferences." In most of these courses there were three lectures per week, and one discussion-group meeting. For each of these General Courses, an elaborate syllabus was prepared containing a running summary of the subject matter of the course and lists of required and supplementary readings. These syllabi were the work of

nouncements, "The College and the Divisions for Sessions of 1943-44."

In the terminology of the University of Chicago, the term *college* was, at first, defined as that administrative and operative part of the University that was primarily concerned with giving an undergraduate a general education. Practically, the College was roughly equivalent to the first half of a four-year college curriculum, the half commonly referred to as an "underclassmen's" program. It is a term equivalent to the term Lower Division in use in the University of California and Stanford University. In 1933, the term College—in University of Chicago usage—was officially extended to include the last two years of high-school and the first two years of university work. In the discussion here, however, the term will be used in the earlier sense, since most undergraduates still enter the University after completing four years of high-school work elsewhere and since the original Chicago College Plan was aimed at such students. (The new program for the "four-year college" will also permit the admission of students from accredited high schools after their graduation and at the beginning of the third year of the College program.) In University of Chicago terminology, the work beyond that of the College is done under one or another of the Divisions, into which the departments are grouped for administrative purposes.

* "The College and the Divisions for the Sessions of 1937-38," *The University of Chicago Announcements,* Vol. XXXVII, No. 7, p. 41.

the group of instructors engaged in the teaching of these courses, and they have undergone repeated careful revision. In the first few years, after the initiation of these courses in 1931, it was customary to invite some of the more distinguished members of the faculty to give occasional lectures in these General Courses. It was found, however, that some of these lecturers performed ineffectively before audiences of two or three hundred underclassmen, and that others who were better performers interrupted the continuity of the course since they were not too familiar with its objectives and procedures. In the main, the work of these courses came to be done by relatively small groups of younger men, constantly in touch with each other and co-operating intellectually in every feature of the work of the course.[9]

The educational procedure in the General Course at the University of Chicago differed in certain other respects from the operation of survey courses elsewhere. "College requirements are stated in terms of educational attainments and *are measured by examinations* which may be taken by the student *whenever he is prepared to take them,* at any scheduled examination period." The only restriction on the time during which these examinations might be taken was that examinations in the four General Courses (plus examinations in two one-year departmental courses and a qualifying examination in English) "must be passed within a period of two years after the first comprehensive examination is passed." * Within this time limit, however, the individual student was responsible for determining for himself when he was ready to come up for a comprehensive examination. The responsibility was further increased by the fact that "regular attendance at classes is not required. Upon examination of the syllabus of a course, a student

* "The College and the Divisions for the Sessions of 1937-38," *The University of Chicago Announcements,* Vol. XXXVII, No. 7, p. 40.

may find that he has mastered certain parts of a course and may advisedly omit the sessions of the class in which these parts are discussed." * Thus the student was encouraged to work by himself and at whatever pace he preferred, provided he passed all the required examinations within the time limits stated above. It was even possible for him to present himself for examination in the subject matter of one of the General Courses in which he had never enrolled as a student.

An essential feature of the Chicago College Plan (as a result of the attempt to make the student more directly responsible for his educational progress) was the emphasis on the passing of comprehensive examinations as marking significant stages in that progress. This emphasis focused the attention of both faculty and students on the examination, its objectives, its techniques, and its validity in the measurement of student accomplishment. Members of the faculty in these General Courses devoted a great deal of time and thought to the preparation of the examinations, and the results—planographed—were made available at a small fee to successive generations of undergraduates.

Each examination is six hours in length, divided into a morning session and an afternoon session. Examination questions are of different types; the ratio of new-type and old-type questions in any given examination is determined by agreement between the instructor and the examiners of the course. Although the construction and administration of the examinations are in the hands of the examination technicians, the objectives and general form of the examinations as well as the materials for the examinations are under the control of the faculty. The Board of Examinations, whose personnel consists in faculty members representing the divisions or schools, employs a Chief Examiner, who selects a staff of technicians and clerks. For each of the four divisions is assigned a special technician, who begins

* *Ibid.*, p. 43.

early in the academic year to consider questions and materials for the examination. Questions are submitted by staff members and discussed in staff meetings; the whole process involves close co-operation between the examiner and those responsible for the teaching of the course.*

The Chicago College Plan in its earlier stages shows obvious resemblances to the Colgate Plan, but the differences are perhaps more significant than the resemblances. The most important difference is the variation in the extent of the survey courses offered under each system. At Colgate, each survey course is limited to a single semester; at Chicago, each survey course ran throughout an academic year. Obviously, undergraduates at Chicago had an opportunity to secure a more thorough orientation in the basic fields of knowledge than Colgate students. Another marked difference is the degree of responsibility imposed upon the individual student. At Colgate, the teaching of the individual student is stressed; at Chicago, the learning by the individual student was emphasized.†

According to Dean Chen, "the most significant aspect of the curriculum pattern is the identification of general education with the understanding of broad fields of knowledge. The four examinations in broad fields and the examination in English, according to Boucher, 'represent a common core of educational experience and background for all students who complete the requirements of our College: they constitute the major part of our definition of the minimum essentials of a general education.' " ‡ Another significant feature is "the individualizing of a fixed cur-

* T.H-E. Chen, *Developing patterns of the college curriculum in the United States,* "Southern California Education Monographs, No. 10" (University of Southern California Press, 1940), pp. 81-82.

† For a more detailed discussion of the pedagogical aspects of the two plans, see Chapter III of this survey.

‡ C. S. Boucher, *The Chicago college plan* (The University of Chicago Press, 1935), p. 20. Quoted in T. H-E. Chen, *op. cit.,* p. 83.

riculum by allowing a student to proceed at his own pace and to map out a program of studies according to his past background and preparation. The product is standardized, but the process is highly individualized."

According to the same observer and critic, the major shortcomings of the Chicago College Plan were the tendency to retain departmental lines in the general courses, the failure to develop an examination program in harmony with the objectives of general education, and its inadequacy in evaluating the non-intellectual phases of student development. "It is, on the whole, fair to say that the entire program at Chicago tends to be predominantly 'academic' in its emphasis. Its stress on intellectual attainments and on 'book learning' tends to result in a neglect of other values important in general education." *

From the point of view of this particular study, the major deficiency of the Chicago College Plan was the overemphasis on the physical, biological, and social sciences, and the underemphasis on the humanities. It is arguable whether or not a program that formalized such an emphasis can be regarded as a satisfactory liberal arts program. The equal weighting of a course involving history, philosophy, religion, literature, music, and the fine arts with a course in any one of the groups of sciences seems on the face of it indefensible. But, aside from this curious evidence as to the contemporary tendency to undervalue the humanities, there is the further—and probably insoluble—problem of creating a year-course in which the numerous and pre-eminently important humanistic disciplines involved shall be satisfactorily presented or effectively synthesized and integrated.[10]

At Scripps College, the desire to furnish students a large amount of common intellectual experience has resulted in

---

* Chen, *op. cit.*, pp. 84-85. For a full consideration by this observer of the Chicago College Plan, see pages 77-83 of the work cited.

the creation of courses in the humanities, required of all students and taking up two-fifths of their time in each of the first three years of their course. This series of courses, in which a large majority of the faculty participate sooner or later, furnishes a basis of intellectual experience for more specialized studies. Moreover, since these courses are required of all students, members of the faculty have the great advantage of being able to assume a very substantial amount of common knowledge on the part of students who have submitted to this discipline. Such a situation offers an agreeable contrast to that of the teacher who does not feel it fair to assume that all his students have had any common intellectual experience other than courses in Freshman English and Hygiene!

The assumptions that underlie the Humanities course at Scripps are suggested by the following remarks of Professor C. L. Barrett:

It has been customary to think of human knowledge as being divided into quite different fields, such as history, literature, art, economics, politics, religion, philosophy, and the sciences. For many purposes such a classification is convenient—and certainly the problems which appear in any one of these fields are more than sufficient to engage the efforts of the specialist for a lifetime. Yet, it would be a serious error to suppose that any final or fundamental separation of the various fields of knowledge is ever possible. In the actual life of every individual and every age, all of these interests are related and each exerts an influence upon the others. Hence, to understand the literature of a period, for example, it becomes necessary to consider its writings in the light of historical events that were transpiring, the economic and political conditions which existed, and the conceptions of art, science, philosophy, and religion that prevailed. Furthermore, since ideas and institutions proceed by a kind of evolutionary development, the attitudes and culture of any age—including one's own—are never really to be understood in isolation from their historical perspective. The specialist who allows his interests to become too narrowly restricted to include the wider relationships of the material he is studying, scarcely may hope to discover the true nature and significance of even his own subject.*

Of the specific objectives of the Humanities course at Scripps, the official interpretation may be cited:

They form essentially an introduction to the development and character of Occidental civilization from ancient to modern times, and are so designed as to unify the student's understanding, familiarize her with the fundamental problems of civilized societies, and suggest interests which she may pursue in detail in the related special courses offered by her instructors. . . . The plan calls for knowledge of a certain number of the most significant facts of human history, but its aim is to pass far beyond any mere concern for events or names and to indicate to the student the bearings of each period of human culture which has entered into the making of our own; in other words, our own *cultural self-understanding* for the better direction of our own lives is the fundamental affair of the Scripps courses in the Humanities.†

The first year of the Scripps Humanities course is devoted to "the study of the earlier formations of our Occidental civilization," particularly, "the gifts to civilization of the Ancient Oriental, and especially the Hebrew culture, and of the Classical, or primarily the Grecian culture . . . The real interest of the course is to acquaint the student with Biblical and Hellenic literatures which form the heart of our own literature, and with the art, music, science, and the moral and religious life that are the ancient sources of our own development." ‡

* *The Humanities Courses, introduction to the syllabus* (Scripps College, 1942-43).
† "Catalogue Number," *Scripps College Bulletin* (1942), Vol. XVI, No. 3, p. 28.
‡ *Ibid.*, p. 29.

The second year of the Scripps Humanities course is devoted to a consideration of Western Civilization up to 1750.

The work of the second year is based on two constant assumptions: (1) that the life of the Western world subsequent to the fifth century A.D. has a common "stream of tendency" and therefore that it has chronological unity; (2) that the changing pattern of its social life is the foundation on which an understanding of its political, intellectual, and artistic achievement should rest. In the largest sense the work of this year forms a course in "polity"—in the study of the causes determining the character of society and the forms of human expression that are the results of these causes.*

The third year of the Scripps Humanities course finds its subject matter in the history of Western Civilization since 1750.

A study of the great powers from the end of the Seven Years' War to the twentieth century, and of the evolution of the modern state and economy, provides the background for the understanding of the main tendencies of ideas both in Europe and in the United States. The study includes the development of the natural sciences and their application to the growth of modern society as well as their repercussion in philosophical thought and human conduct. . . . Although the course is based upon the political and social history, its emphasis is laid on the personalities representing the achievements of the age in the world of spiritual creation. The writings of these men form an important part of the required reading. A brief survey of the classical and romantic music and a selection of lectures on art and architecture correlate the domain of music and the fine arts with the attempted synoptic view of the two centuries of modern civilization which are the immediate foundation of our own life.†

* "Catalogue Number," Vol. XVI, No. 3, p. 30.
† *Ibid.*, pp. 31-32.

46

The particular distinctions of the Scripps Humanities course arise from three factors: the length of time devoted to it, the amount of time it occupies in the student's program, and the even distribution of emphasis over the various elements in the humanistic field—history, philosophy, religion, literature, music, and the fine arts. The length of time devoted to this course and its prominence in the student's four-year program go a very considerable distance in offsetting the objection frequently made to courses in Western European Civilization extending through a single college year—namely, that such a course must inevitably be superficial and that it can give the student only a trivial acquaintance with a large number of very complex phenomena. The distribution of emphasis over the various constituent elements of the humanities meets another frequently encountered objection, namely, that such courses tend to interpret history in a narrow political or military or dynastic sense and that they are likely to give an inadequate amount of attention to the intellectual, spiritual, and esthetic aspects of the great epochs with which they deal. It must be confessed that in the hands of most historians the aspects just mentioned are likely to be neglected. This contingency is avoided in the Scripps Humanities system by the fact that the course is given not by historians but by a committee of men trained in the different disciplines involved in any well-balanced presentation of the cultures of complex human epochs. Perhaps the most serious charge that may be made against the Scripps plan is that, hitherto at least, it has not given sufficient weight, apparently, to the contribution of science to human history. The inability of Scripps to present this aspect of human-culture history adequately is perhaps a reflection of the way in which American scientists are trained, rather than a reflection on the way in which American humanists are trained.[11]

The interdepartmental courses and programs described

in this chapter have developed in response to a dissatisfaction with the educational results of the elective system and of highly departmental schedules. The common element in these programs is their deliberate and systematic crossing of departmental boundaries. The programs differ in their extent and complexity. The simplest form is the one-semester or full-year course in which two or more departments co-operate. When a series of such courses is required of all undergraduates—as in the Chicago College Plan, the Colgate Plan, and the Scripps Humanities Courses—there is obviously the conviction that it is desirable that undergraduates should share a rather extensive intellectual experience. In interdepartmental programs running throughout the undergraduate course—such as the Divisional Humanities Program at Princeton and the School of Humanities Program at Stanford—an attempt is made to integrate the whole, or almost the whole, of the undergraduate's intellectual experience by assisting him in discovering a significant cultural pattern in it.

CHAPTER III

EXPERIMENTATION IN THE TECHNIQUES OF TEACHING

ONE of the most striking features of the educational procedures of our time is the widespread experimentation with techniques of teaching. Accordingly, this chapter will be devoted to classifying and describing some of these techniques and suggesting their values and deficiencies. Since these experiments need to be set against the background of conventional teaching methods in liberal arts colleges and universities, an attempt will first be made to describe the traditional techniques and to indicate why it has seemed advisable to break away from them or at least to modify them.

The normal teaching technique in the field of the humanities is a combination of lectures, readings, recitations, papers, quizzes, and final examinations. In this combination, the lecture is commonly regarded as the most important of the devices used; at least, it is the central device among these devices and the one that is considered the foundation-stone of the whole educational experience.[1] Good, bad, or indifferent; carelessly or carefully organized; formally or informally delivered; a causerie, a dramatic monologue, or an oration, the lecture is still the *piece de resistance* of the academic feast—at least to the appetite of the professor.

The professor's appetite for giving lectures is so definitely insatiable that it may be worth while to raise the question as to the reasons for this overdevelopment of a normal impulse. Anyone who has had even a brief experience in academic society knows the risk he runs of being lectured to on every possible occasion. Certainly one of the reasons why faculty meetings are one of the major forms of torture a citizen in academic society must face is the professor's habit of setting forth his ideas at length whenever and wherever there is anyone who must reluctantly listen. The professor's passion for oral expression finds its sources perhaps in the fact that, at least in the humanities and the social sciences, his subject matter condemns him to deal constantly with verbal symbols, and, in the second place, in the fact that years of lecturing have established a deep-rooted habit of verbalizing. Possibly the symbolic nature of mathematics tends to make mathematicians the most verbal of scientists, and the concrete nature of the laboratory sciences, on the other hand, may explain the relatively silent introverted laboratory-type of scientist. Another reason for the professor's addiction to lecturing is the fact that it is, by all odds, the easiest of the educational techniques to apply. It demands no contact with the students' minds; it requires no adjustment to the students' ignorance or knowledge. In most institutions, it raises no question as to whether or not the student has any desire to hear the lecture. It does not require any expertness in the techniques of question and answer, much less of genuine intellectual discussion. For the often psychologically insecure academic type, the lecture method is ideal for the establishment, not only of a sense of security but also of a sense of superiority, since he assumes—without examination—that he is addressing his intellectual inferiors. The college furnishes the classroom and the audience and invests him with professorial authority. His only task is to open the spigot of verbalism and keep the stream flowing until, or after, the bell rings.

To the student the lecture is probably the major source

of information concerning the subject matter of the course. From it, rather than from any of the other sources of information, he expects to "get the dope," because it is likely to be the most reliable index, not only to what the professor regards as important but also to what the student is most likely to be asked to return to the professor in quizzes and final examinations. In consequence, the student feels that a reasonably full record of the professor's lectures is a better guide to what he is expected to know than the most expertly planned and written textbook on the subject.

The dependence on the lecture as the major method of instruction in college education is perhaps the most striking feature of the conventional technique of higher education. Until recently, its primary place in that technique has rarely been questioned, and certainly among most professorial lecturers there has been little inclination to question the rationale of the lecture or to investigate its functions. Certainly, its persistence as the primary mode of instruction is due to the combined influences of tradition and academic inertia rather than to any burning conviction as to its superiority to other techniques of teaching.

Regarded historically, the modern classroom lecture is a lineal descendant of the system of lecturing developed in the Middle Ages in an era when books were few and very expensive. In that period, the lecture was the substitute for the textbook, as it very frequently is in the minds of many students today. Justified in a period when books were scarce, it has continued to exist in a period when books are relatively cheap and when many other methods of instruction are available. At its worst, the contemporary academic lecture is little more than a running summary of the textbook being studied. On a somewhat higher level, the lecture may represent a fairly skillful synthesis of what the professor knows about the subject of his discourse, and thus it has the value of furnishing a lucid condensation and exposition of facts and ideas garnered from wide reading and experience. At its best, the lecture may furnish the student a fresh and stimulating view of familiar subject matter.

But it is certainly pertinent to ask whether or not the lecture deserves its primary position among the techniques of academic education. Should it retain its primacy over even such conventional methods as the recitation, the paper, the quiz, and the final examination, not to mention the newer devices which it is the purpose of this chapter to consider? Does not the use of the lecture as a pedagogical technique rest upon an unsound conception of the educational process or at least upon one that requires serious qualification? [2]

The theory upon which not only the lecture and the recitation but most quizzes and final examinations rest is the theory that it is the teacher's function to educate the student, not that it is the student's responsibility to educate himself. This theory rests on the assumption that the student's mind is blank or nearly so and that the teacher makes, by one or another device, some sort of recording on the student's mind, which the student should be able to reproduce in quizzes or final examinations but which he is not to be asked to reproduce, once the final examination has been written. Or the teacher regards the mind of the student as a sponge which he attempts to saturate by dripping information upon it—information which he expects to get back, in a somewhat murky state, by squeezing the student's mind by the constrictive devices of quizzes and examinations. Throughout this experience, the good student is the passive, docile, and recipient one, and not the active, aggressive, challenging, and critical one.

The results attained by the conventional educational processes just outlined have been to many observers and students so disappointing that there have developed during

52

the last two or three decades a number of experiments with other pedagogical techniques. One of the most revealing studies—the Pennsylvania survey conducted by the Carnegie Foundation for the Advancement of Teaching—has shown the startling consequences of putting all college students through the conventional academic mill. The performance of 1,503 high-school seniors—unselected students of average quality—5,747 college sophomores, and 3,720 college seniors on the "same test of certain essentials of general education," brought the following results:

Although the average score (314) of the college seniors is much higher than that of the sophomores (254), 28.4 per cent of the seniors, or 1,058 individuals, do less well than the average sophomore, and nearly ten per cent do less well than the average high-school senior. So also the average high-school senior score (178) is below the college-sophomore level (254), but 22 per cent of this secondary-school group surpass it and exactly ten per cent, or 150 pupils, exceed the college-senior average (314).[3]

What is indicated by this study and other studies of the results of the conventional liberal arts education training . is that that training must be radically revised if it is to secure more favorable results. The techniques and devices to be discussed in this chapter all seem to find their *raison d'être* in the desire to discover methods that will attain such more favorable results. Whatever their nature, and however timorous or radical they may be in their violation or abandonment of conventional practices, they are at one in their attempt to insure the individual student's getting more out of his educational experience than the conventional lecture-recitation-examination system has given him. In each and every one of them, there is a marked increase in the attention paid the individual student, his aptitudes, his limitations, his interests, and deficiency in interests.

Perhaps the most common deviation from the lecture-recitation-examination system is the use of the comprehensive examination as a pedagogical device. This deviation has now become almost conventional in the procedures of liberal arts colleges. Normally, the comprehensive examination is the crowning effort of the undergraduate in the conclusion of his major program. Normally, the comprehensive examination is intended to "cover the field" of the major and to indicate the extent to which the student has covered the field. Of this academic innovation, R. F. Butts writes: "Harvard was early engaged in this field of comprehensive examinations; Chicago has developed them to a great extent; and a number of other colleges have adopted them in greater or lesser degree. In recent years, many educators have urged that the factual nature of tests and measurements should give way to a greater emphasis on 'evaluation' techniques of a broader kind to help the student develop more genuinely in all aspects of his personal and social life." *

The precise objectives of the comprehensive examination are probably not very clear, even to faculty members who devote hours to the composition of such examinations and even more hours to grading them.[4] The general objective of the comprehensive examination is, it would probably be agreed, the attempt to discover what sort of control a student has over a body of material accumulated in connection with a series of disparate courses in the major field. It is probably true that most comprehensive examinations concentrate their efforts on discovering the quantity of the student's information relevant to the field in which he is majoring. It is extremely doubtful whether most comprehensive examinations test much more than the ability to retain in memory—for at least the period of the

* R. F. Butts, *The college charts its course* (McGraw-Hill, 1939), p. 413.

54

examination—a considerable number of facts and the ability to present those facts with a moderate degree of orderliness and clarity of expression. Certainly most liberal arts colleges have made very little use of the new techniques of examination now common in secondary-school procedure. The liberal arts professor generally is exceedingly suspicious of any mechanical devices intended to measure a student's information, knowledge, or intellectual quality. The testing method in most comprehensive examinations is the essay-type examination—a type that it has been conclusively demonstrated is impossible of exact evaluation. Certain colleges and universities, better oriented in testing methods, now use a combination of objective and essay questions with satisfactory results.

Institutions vary widely in their offering of guidance in preparation for comprehensive examinations. At Wesleyan University, where conventional pedagogical procedures predominate, the seniors preparing for the comprehensive examination meet on one evening each week with some member of the department giving the examination. The purpose of this meeting is the discussion of certain authors and texts from the reading list on which the comprehensive is based. It is assumed—frequently on inadequate grounds—that the seniors have read the texts to be discussed at each meeting. All too often the meeting deteriorates into a high-powered cram session on the texts supposedly under discussion. The series of "comprehensive" meetings has the value, however, of furnishing all seniors in the group a sort of sight-seeing tour of the major monuments in the field in which they are majoring, and it undoubtedly accounts for the fact that seniors who have taken this tour have a commendable familiarity with at least the surfaces of the monuments they have seen. It is also a consequence of this system that questions on comprehensive examinations are likely to make no much heavier demand upon the students than the memory, in considerable detail, of the content of the works read or discussed. Questions demanding a really searching knowledge of the texts or a close comment on the technical or esthetic aspects of the works are likely to be debarred from the examination as too closely resembling "course-questions."

The educational "bottle-feeding" that is implicit in the system just described is absent from the comprehensive examination system in vogue at Chicago. There the student is supposed to prepare himself for the examination, and the kinds of training in which he is expected to show skills are clearly indicated in the announcements of the Departments. In the survey courses he is supposed to prepare himself for the examination with the aid of lectures, discussion groups, and private reading and study.

The requirements for the Bachelor's degree at Chicago are met by passing comprehensive examinations—rather than by earning credit in individual courses. When a student has completed his preparation in a subject, either by formal class instruction or by independent study (a student is not required to register for a course to admit him to an examination), he takes an examination prepared by a group of instructors with the assistance of the staff of the University Examiner. The papers are read anonymously and are graded by readers other than the instructor in the course. In this way all considerations except the student's mastery of the subject and his ability to think clearly about it are eliminated. Students are not rewarded for having made a good personal impression on an instructor or for having memorized his favorite ideas or phrases, nor are they penalized for having failed to do these things.*

According to this system, the student realizes that the responsibility for preparing himself for a comprehensive

* "The College and the Divisions for Sessions of 1943-44," *The University of Chicago Announcements*, pp. 47-48.

examination rests squarely on his own shoulders and that neither lectures nor discussion groups nor individual conferences are intended primarily to coach him for these examinations. Of this assignment of responsibility to the student, Professor E. G. Bewkes of Colgate University has written:

Chicago appears to be committed to the idea that as an educational enterprise it exists for the purpose of providing opportunities for those who can appreciate and profit from them. There is no compulsion, no required attendance. The plant is available, the professors are functioning, the university has done its part, let the student now do his.*

The comprehensive examinations given at the University of Chicago are very formidable affairs. They are six hours in length, and cover the work to which the average student is supposed to devote a third or a fourth of his time during a period of nine months. They utilize various objective and visual devices along with questions of the "short-essay" type.†

On the whole, the device of the comprehensive examination marks a very distinct advance in educational procedure. If it has no other result, it discourages the student's habit—which the elective system and the course-credit system have encouraged—of regarding his education as the

* E. G. Bewkes, *Observations on Chicago and Colgate plans* (a report to the faculty of Colgate University), p. 4.

† Despite the length and complexity of these examinations, during a period of six years I never heard from University of Chicago students any complaint about the arduousness of clearing these academic hurdles. Possibly one reason for the absence of complaints was the fact that the students knew that they were graded on a sliding scale and not on some scale of indeterminate perfection. In other words, of six hundred students taking a single course, a very large number could count on, at least, passing the examination. The most difficult problem of grading was perhaps that of determining where the line between passing and failure was to be drawn. This system, whatever its disadvantages, has the advantage of measuring the student's achievement against the achievement of the whole group being examined.

accumulation of credits for work done in separate, distinct, and unrelated courses, and of considering education as an accumulative rather than a synthesizing intellectual activity. It encourages the student in trying to see his major subject as a whole, in trying to get an overview of it and to discover significant patterns in it. Altogether too frequently, however, the student is left to himself to achieve this overview and naturally ends by relying on third-rate texts and cramming guides instead of on professors whose guidance might be superior to that of the writers of cheap guides to knowledge. Probably the most serious shortcoming of the comprehensive examination system is that neither the teacher nor the taught is clearly conscious of its objectives or of the demands that it ought to make upon both these agents to education. Certainly if the comprehensive examination is to be the crowning effort of the student's undergraduate career, he ought to be given specific indications of what sorts of things are to be tested by this ordeal. Of this matter under the present system, neither the teacher nor the taught is likely to be very certain.[5]

The remaining experimental teaching techniques to be described and discussed fall broadly into two groups: those that are accessories or appendages to more or less conventional educational methods, and those that are divorced almost entirely from such conventional methods.

Experimentation of the first general sort can again be divided into two types: group activities subsidiary to the lecture system and individual activities that go on independently of the lecture system but are concurrent with it.

Of student group activities subsidiary to the lecture system, perhaps the first to appear on the stage of American higher education was the Princeton preceptorial system. According to this system, each of the lectures in a course is followed up by one or two meetings of a small group with the professor who has given the lecture or with one of his mature colleagues who is assisting him. The preceptorial meeting is devoted, not to an elucidation of the material presented in the lecture but to a discussion of the reading assigned in connection with it. The preceptorial group includes from five to ten students, and this size not only makes possible an intimate view of the personality of each of the student-members of the group but also gives each student an opportunity to express himself freely and to engage in discussion with his intellectual equals, since the function of the preceptor is that of guiding the discussion rather than that of systematic cross-examination with the intention of proving the student guilty of stupidity, ignorance, or willful neglect of duty. The method also necessitates the students' more or less close contact with the text under discussion, their analysis of it in order to distinguish the more important from the less important ideas in it, and a critical consideration of the validity of these ideas. The preceptorial system has the value also of giving students practice in the informal but free expression of their ideas in a situation more relaxed than that of the classroom recitation.

The effective operation of the preceptorial system is not easy but it is not so difficult that it could not be learned by any except the most voluble and dictatorial members of the faculty. In this system, as in almost any other academic system, the tempting way out of the real pedagogical difficulty is for the teacher to do more than his share of the work, and to turn the preceptorial meeting into a little lecture. Even when this temptation is not resisted, there are definite gains intrinsic to the system in the intimacy of the relationship between the teacher and the taught, in the encouragement to expressiveness on the part of the students, and in the possible training it gives in fairly close reading of texts.

The discussion-group method is analogous to the preceptorial, and may in fact be regarded as the best compromise a large university can make between the desire to reach the individual student's mind on the oral level and the fact of the large numbers with which universities have to deal, at least in introductory courses. The typical status of the discussion group is that of an adjunct to the lectures to large student audiences characteristic of the survey courses now fairly common at least in the larger universities. Thus, at the University of Chicago, the Humanities course in its earlier stages (1931-38) was conducted by means of lectures, readings, and discussion groups. "Three lectures a week outline in chronological order the political and institutional setting of each of the main cultural phases through which Western civilization has passed, and indicate the characteristic achievements of each period in thought and in literary and artistic expression. The collateral reading is directed very largely to actual masterpieces of thought and literature of the past. Each discussion group is focused on a particular book or limited group of reproductions of works of art. By direct contact with the creations of philosophers, poets, and artists the effort is made to stimulate imagination, appreciation, and critical judgment." *

It would seem obvious that the difficulties of conducting a discussion group satisfactorily are far greater than those of conducting a preceptorial group successfully. With a discussion group numbering twenty-five or thirty, there is a temptation to turn the discussion into a recitation in order to discover whether or not the students have read the assignments. There is the added difficulty of getting a relatively equal expressiveness from all the members of a group of this size. Every teacher will be familiar with

* "The College and the Divisions," *The University of Chicago Announcements*, Vol. XXXVII, No. 7, p. 47.

the temptation—at least on his less energetic days—to allow the more expressive members of the class to carry the burden of the discussion and to allow the shyer and less expressive members to "doodle" on the margins of their notebooks.

The early stage of the Chicago system raises the further and more important question of the relative emphasis on lectures and discussions in large survey courses. The proportion of three lectures to one discussion group suggests the consideration that the theory of the student as a passive recipient of instruction still dominates the minds of the operators of such courses. Two reasons may be suggested for the persistence of this proportion. One is the practical consideration that the teaching-load involved in the giving of three lectures a week is incomparably lighter than the teaching-load involved in the conducting of, say, twenty discussion-groups meeting twice a week. The other consideration is the fact that it is easier to lecture to a group of two or three hundred students than it is to conduct as many as four discussion groups covering the same literary or pictorial works of art.*

The proportion of lectures to discussion-group meetings in the Stanford University course in the History of Western Civilization would seem to go much further in individualizing the educational process and in bringing about a fairly intimate contact between the mind of the teacher and the mind of the student. "The course is organized on the basis of one lecture and three section meetings each week. The lectures . . . are designed to supply informa-

* In the Humanities Course at Scripps College, the same proportion is apparent—three lectures per week and one discussion group. Since the course is planned to occupy two-fifths of the student's time instead of a fourth, as at Chicago, the proportion of lectures to discussion-groups at Scripps is perhaps slightly more defensible. In the later stages of the Humanities course at Chicago, the number of lectures, it is significant to note, has been very considerably lessened, and the number of discussion-group meetings correspondingly increased.

61

tion, interpretation, illustrative material related to the week's reading and discussions . . . The preliminary statement for the work of each week is designed to offer, not a fixed delimitation of the subject matter, but merely an introductory survey for the better orientation of the student. The notes on the source reading suggest the relation of these readings to the general narrative; map questions call for a study of essential geographical data; the lists of questions offer suggestive points of departure for discussion and a basis for self-testing on the part of the student.[6]

To the fairly common practice of combining one or more lectures with one or more discussion groups a week in survey courses in the humanities, the practice at Colgate University is an exception. At this institution, two semester courses cover material embraced in the humanities, one devoted to Philosophy and Religion and the other to Literature and the Fine Arts. In these survey courses, and in the other required survey courses at Colgate, the following is the practice: "The survey classes meet four times a week in small groups of not more than eighteen to a class. Occasionally there may be a general lecture or the showing of moving pictures, such as those developed at the University of Chicago, the Bureau of Mines, etc." * There is an obvious advantage here in the intimacy of the contact between the teacher and the taught and in the opportunity for the student to take an active part in his own education rather than to serve as a passive recipient of it. There is almost certainly a loss in the fact that each discussion group throughout the semester is taught by a single instructor. Accordingly, each group gets one man's view of the material presented in the textbook that com-

* E. G. Bewkes, "The Colgate Plan," in *General education* (1934), Vol. VI, p. 113.

prises most or all of the reading required for the course. Thus, the survey course in Philosophy and Religion concentrates on the text produced for the course. The individual student, therefore, gets one man's interpretation of the text rather than various views or composite views of the material under discussion. The student, moreover, under this system is not protected from the tendency of the teacher to expound and elaborate the text instead of discovering the student's understanding of the text and his reaction to it.*

It is fortunate that we have a judgment of the survey courses under the Colgate system and under the Chicago system in its earlier phases. Professor E. G. Bewkes, who is in charge of the survey courses at Colgate, presented a report to the faculty on these two systems, and from it I have permission to quote:

The method of giving these beginning courses is quite different. At Chicago there are three general lectures per week to the entire group in each of the four introductory courses, and then one class hour in each course. The class hour is a conference or clearance hour. Each student is assigned to a class section, and there are not more than twenty-five assigned to any one group. Attendance, as at the lectures, is optional.

At Colgate, on the other hand, the general lecture idea was given up, after experiment, in favor of small groups of not more than eighteen in a group, meeting four times a week. A great deal of individual attention is possible in groups of this size.†

---

* From the discussion groups I visited in connection with this study, I came away with the feeling that the teachers had given vivid and even brilliant personal performances but that the performances of the students—the supporting cast—were negligible because of the star-system that seemed to dominate the production. After all, a discussion group ought to bring out the quality of the students rather than the quality of the professor.

† E. G. Bewkes, *Observations on Chicago and Colgate plans* (a report to the faculty of Colgate University), p. 5.

Of the relative values of the lecture-discussion-group system and the discussion-group system without lectures, Professor Bewkes writes:

We cannot help feeling that there is danger of impersonalism in the Chicago concept of its relation to the student; while Chicago thinks we have gone too far in this direction. After all, the student is so much more than a recipient of intellectual opportunities. It is doubtful whether we should assume the maturity that the Chicago plan requires. Even though there may be intellectual maturity, the student at the freshman stage is still a plastic youngster. It is the Colgate view that its emphasis on frequent individual contact, within the small Survey groups, and by the preceptorial relation and later by the tutorial relation, will probably do more to develop the individual as a whole, as well as to develop him as a competent student within a field of knowledge.*

Another attempt to individualize the educational process is the provision of some means by which the student may have a more or less informal individual contact with a member of the faculty and individual supervision of a portion of his work. This provision for individual study seems to have grown out of the conviction that, in larger institutions particularly, the contacts of the student with individual members of the faculty and of the faculty with individual students were distressingly infrequent and that the growth in the size of classes had brought about the decline in a productive kind of faculty-student contact characteristic of the smaller institutions.

Three examples of this technique, intended to create informal contacts between the faculty and individual students, may be cited by way of illustration.

The Independent Study Plan at Stanford is one of the most carefully planned and systematically conducted of

* E. G. Bewkes, *op. cit.*, p. 8. On the Colgate preceptorial-tutorial system, see below.

these experiments, and its operation and results have been described by Professor E. E. Robinson in a report entitled *Independent study in the lower division of Stanford University, 1931-37.*

Of the aim of the Independent Study Plan, Professor Robinson writes:

The primary aim of all independent study has been to stimulate the superior student to do more work and better work than he would ordinarily do without individual supervision. The superior student finds himself in an unfavorable situation when he is placed in a class with the majority of students with whom he can compete without full effort . . . It has been the desire of those in charge of independent study to provide for the student of liberal studies such conditions that he will be led to work with the determination and the interest of the professional student at the program agreed upon as his own.*

The techniques used in the Independent Study Plan seem to be adaptations of the tutorial system characteristic of Oxford and Cambridge. The "three consciously used devices" have been reading, writing, and "oral presentations." Of the last, Professor Robinson writes:

Most important of all, what the student has had to say about his reading and his thinking has found direct expression in discussion which has not been "recitation." It has been thought that ability to express in speech his ideas, whether factual or critical, should be of primary concern to the student.†

Both in the preliminary stages of the operation of the Independent Study Plan at Stanford and during the period particularly discussed by Professor Robinson, the work was an adjunct to the regular course work of the student.

* E. E. Robinson, *Independent study in the lower division of Stanford University, 1931-37* (Stanford University Press, 1937), p. 11.
† *Ibid.*, p. 13.

The plan of study was arranged with the intention of providing, in addition to courses which the student might elect, a program of work both more comprehensive and more intensive than that of the average student, calling for greater initiative, more self-direction, and a higher type of thinking, and leading to a comprehensive final examination.*

Of the results of this program a committee of the faculty reported:

The individual-study student achieves a more rapid and more vigorous growth, a greater intellectual maturity, a more sustained interest, a more acute awareness of the significance of the subject, and a greater skill and economy in the management of time, effort, and materials of study.†

The committee also reported that there had been a distinct improvement in the motivation and the quality of reading and writing. Students had tended to read whole books and not merely fragments of books. They had, moreover, developed the habit of reading works of primary importance rather than third-rate textbooks giving accounts of such works.‡

The functions of the tutor under the system operative at Harvard are somewhat similar to those of the faculty engaged in the Independent Study Plan at Stanford. According to the Harvard system, the tutors "will aid the students in correlating the work of their courses, and will seek especially to develop in them habits of profitable reading, independent thinking, and scholarly methods. It is not the Tutor's function, however, to serve as a coach for the

*E. E. Robinson, *op. cit.*, p. 8. From 1925-31, the Independent Study Plan applied only to juniors and seniors; after 1931, it was extended to include freshmen and sophomores.
†*Ibid.*, p. 66.
‡For a fuller account of the faculty's and the students' estimation of this program, see Robinson, *op. cit.*, pp. 63-73.

General Examinations." * Tutorial work at Harvard begins in the sophomore year, and continues, with varying degrees of intensity, during the remainder of the student's course. In the department of English, the subject matter of the tutorial is selected from among the fields or topics on which the student will be tested in the departmental section of the General Examination. The tutorial, therefore, would seem to take the place of one or more courses on the student's program each year, and the method seems to aim, not merely at the objectives stated above, but also at personalizing the student's instruction and at furnishing some ground for fairly close contact between the student and at least one member of the faculty. For each of the fields or topics selected for tutorial study, reading lists are provided which are, in some cases at least, more extensive and far-reaching than the required reading lists in courses on these subjects.

At Colgate University, distinction is made between the personalized instruction given a student during his freshman year and that given him during his sophomore year. The member of the faculty to whom the freshman is assigned is called a preceptor. The member of the faculty to whom the sophomore is assigned is called a tutor. The preceptor's functions would seem to be dual: first, that of the conventional college adviser, and, second, that of the student's intellectual mentor. Professor E. G. Bewkes has described the functions of the preceptor as follows:

We would emphasize that this is not a revival of the old advisory system. On the contrary, the preceptorial relation is an integral part of the educational plan. To be sure, the preceptor must study his student, but not solely or primarily in the capacity of problem adjuster, though personal adjustment situations may arise and be dealt with. The preceptor con-

* "Rules Relating to College Studies," *Official Register of Harvard University*, Vol. XXXVI, No. 8, p. 6.

siders the student from the standpoint of his intellectual life taken as a whole. The preceptor seeks to discover and uncover intellectual aptitudes and interests, and then reading assignments are made which are actually read and discussed in the weekly preceptorial hour . . . Intellectual problems, doubts, and attitudes come into the open, and new facts and considerations through reading and discussion are brought into view. Out of such contact, of course, comes confidence and friendship with its many indirect possibilities of attaining ends which older advisory systems sought, but did not find.*

The sophomore's tutor has the function of orienting the student in the field in which he has decided to concentrate. He is a member of the staff of the School (or Division) in which the student is planning to begin his concentration.

The relation is definitely tutorial, dealing with reading matter and discussion within the field of concentration. This work points in the direction of that comprehension which, two years hence, is to be tested by the comprehensive examination. The Sophomore tutorial relation is thus much more particularized in intent than the Freshman preceptorial relation, which is more general. Nevertheless, the Sophomore tutorial may include and accomplish incidentally much that was achieved by the earlier relationship.†

Honors work, which has now become a feature of the educational offerings of many American colleges, usually involves a good deal of tutorial work.[7] The general objective of Honors work, however, is not merely the personalizing of college instruction, but the encouragement of high-grade students to undertake programs of individual and more or less independent study which will develop powers their more mediocre companions presumably do not have. As already indicated in our discussion

* E. G. Bewkes, "The Colgate Plan," *General education* (1934), Vol. VI, p. 114.
† Bewkes, *op. cit.*, p. 115.

of Honors programs in an earlier chapter, the objective of Honors work may be an intensification of the student's departmental work or an extension of his intellectual experience through the development of relationships between his own department and other related departments. In the former case, techniques are chosen that will have the effect of intensifying the student's knowledge of his field and also of training him in mature and independent manipulation of the materials in his field. In addition to a more or less close tutorial supervision, the most popular techniques connected with Honors work are the thesis and the Honors examination. At Harvard, the thesis required of Honors students in English "should ordinarily be between 7,500 and 10,000 words." Whether or not the student receives Honors, high Honors, or highest Honors, depends on his showing in the General Examination, in the thesis, and in a special oral examination. In the more general field of literature, the thesis, of not more than 10,000 words, is on a subject involving the study of both ancient and modern literature.

Certain institutions have adapted the educational technique of the thesis to all candidates for the bachelor's degree. At Princeton University, each student in the Department of English,

in conference with his supervisor, must select a thesis topic and a field of independent reading for senior year chosen from the following: 1, Drama; 2, Lyric and reflective poetry; 3, Narrative poetry; 4, Prose fiction; 5, The history of literary criticism; 6, The classical tradition; 7, American literature; 8, The English language. During the senior year he will prepare a thesis, or long essay, to be submitted not later than four weeks after the beginning of the Spring Term. . . . The subject of this essay will ordinarily lie within the field of his independent reading, and must have the approval of his supervisor and of the committee in charge. . . . The essay must deal with a significant author, or with one of the more important aspects of English literature.*

At Reed College, a senior thesis is also one of the requirements of most of the departments in the humanities and the social sciences. In both cases, I have the impression that students are expected to work independently of faculty direction or supervision, and, in all probability, the educational experience involved is valuable. The results vary, of course, in effectiveness and quality in accordance not only with the student's capacities but also with the care with which his department has prepared him for carrying out a sustained piece of carefully organized, expressed, and documented writing. Certainly superior students find the experience of preparing and completing such a piece of work a valuable test of their powers of independent application and of their intellectual efficiency.†

Both tutorial work and Honors work are, in general, methods of personalized instruction. At Princeton, the Divisional Program in the Humanities, some aspects of which have already been discussed in Chapter II, shows an interesting and promising combination of individual and group instruction. Since the thesis cuts across two or more fields in the Humanities, the student not only works under the direction of the Divisional Committee member from his particular department, but has the advice and comfort of

---

* *Official Register of Princeton University*, Vol. XXXIV, No. 1, p. 148.

† It is significant perhaps that the replies to a questionnaire sent out to former Honors students by President J. L. McConaughy of Wesleyan University indicated that an overwhelming majority regarded the preparation of their Honors thesis as the most profitable part of their work for an Honors degree. This evidence is the more striking in that Wesleyan undergraduates, in the main, have little or no experience in the preparation of very extended papers until they face the problem of writing an Honors thesis.

70

members of the Divisional Committee in other departments. In addition, all the students working under the Divisional Program are assembled at various stages of their educational experience for a series of conferences on topics particularly pertinent to each stage of their development.

A conference in freshman year introduces them to the general aims and methods of the Program. In sophomore year a series of conferences is held on the nature of evidence and interpretation. Each of the six members of the Committee gives one or more lectures on this common topic from the point of view of his own subject, and the students discuss with them assigned reading in the general field and in this or that more restricted area. These conferences seek to instill a strong sense of fact, and of the principles of evidence by which fact can be established; they also seek to show the need for meaningful interpretation, and the ways in which interpretation varies with historical conditions and philosophical conceptions. The emphasis throughout on common features of humanistic study and on the points of contact between the departments of instruction helps the student, at an early stage in his college course, to avoid excessive departmentalism and to plan a unified course of study in his upperclass years. In junior year a conference is held on the technique of writing a humanistic thesis, and in senior year several conferences are devoted to the critical exploration of problems specifically related to the subjects on which the students are writing.*

This system of conferences in which all the members of the Divisional Committee and all the students working under the Program participate goes a considerable distance in building up a valuable common intellectual experience in a group slowly developing a deeply humanistic point of view.

* Quoted from a statement of Princeton University's Divisional Committee in the Humanities.

The most spectacular modification of pedagogical procedures in the liberal arts college has resulted from the extension into certain experimental colleges of the educational principles associated with the "progressive education" movement. The central originating idea of this movement is the belief that the school should be child-centered, and not faculty-centered; in other words, that the program and methods of the school should grow out of the nature and needs of the student and should not be determined by the experience of the faculty and by their conception of what the program and methods and material ought to be.[8] Under this system, the child is the focus of attention, and his interests and needs determine not only his activities but those of his teachers.[9] In American higher education, this shifting of focus from the teacher to the taught is revolutionary, and there is no wonder that the results of this shift have been viewed with distaste, if not apprehension, by persons habituated to the older philosophies of education. For the assumptions that underlie this shift are widely at variance with the more or less unconscious assumptions that underlie the procedures of the conventional liberal arts college. The administrations and faculties of institutions of the latter type seem to operate on what President Cowley of Hamilton College calls the "natural depravity" theory, the conviction that human nature is naturally bad, that the nature of youth is weak, if not vicious, and that education is the process of forcing the child, willy-nilly, into the straitjacket of civilized human behavior and of the characteristic culture of his class. From this "natural depravity" theory spring many of the procedures, disciplinary and pedagogical, of the conventional liberal arts college: the elaborate systems of prohibitions and admonitions with regard to attendance at class and chapel, presence on or off the campus, classroom manners, and standards of performance.[10] This theory depends in part on the assumption that the child is naturally hostile to education and that he must be forced, by fair means or foul, to acquire it. Perhaps the most distressing result of this theory is the implication that the ideal student is the one who receives passively and without dispute the instruction imparted to him by an incessantly voluble lecturer.[11] Under this system the rewards go to the docile and unargumentative, the passive, dependent, and unadventurous. It is one of the anomalies of the conventional American system that the college attempts to inculcate in young males the apron-string virtues of passivity, dependence, and docility.[12]

It is even more ironical that the colleges of which the principles of student-centered education are the foundation are, for the most part, colleges for young women, perhaps, as President Constance Warren of Sarah Lawrence College says, because "fathers want their sons to have a *good* education, but don't care what kind of education their daughters have." Whatever be the reason, the fact remains that the best illustrations of student-centered colleges are such experimental institutions as Sarah Lawrence College, founded in 1928, and its sister college, Bennington, founded in 1932. Of the principles that underlie the older institution, Miss Warren writes:

Within the past decade several colleges have been organized, or reorganized, with a new approach to the old problem of what educates . . . In essence, all subscribe to the same underlying educational philosophy. Its emphasis is on the individual and on what happens to him or her in the process we call education.

Each student, we believe, has within herself the seeds of what she is capable of becoming. The purpose of her college education is to enable the student to develop these innate powers to their utmost and grow into a mature individual,

73

emotionally and intellectually capable of coming to terms with whatever life may have in store for her.

What is the essence of the new approach to education? It is individualized education, adapted to the different capacities, interests, and objectives of individual students, to the best of the faculty's ability to understand, recognize and satisfy such differing needs. The curriculum must be flexible to serve individual ends, and cannot be considered as an end in itself, or a straitjacket to fit all alike. We are convinced that the student's desire to learn is fully as important as her innate ability; one with ordinary ability and strong motivation will often accomplish more than another with superior talent who lacks that vital spark.

First aid to this type of education is skilled individual guidance founded on sympathetic understanding of adolescent confusions. It is not pampering or spoon-feeding. It is an honest endeavor to put into practice all that modern psychology can teach us about the learning process, to clear the road of obstacles, and to set the student free.*

In order to encourage the individual's independent pursuit of her own education, such colleges as Sarah Lawrence and Bennington have made essential modifications in the conventional college procedures. In the first place, each student normally takes three courses a year, instead of the usual four or five. In the second place, each of these courses usually meets for a single long session once a week. The procedure in such a seminar is described thus:

The group is small, generally not more than ten or twelve, and the students sit with the instructor informally about a table. During this period, the instructor may challenge them to examine their prejudices, their stock responses; to look into their own backgrounds for materials bearing on the educational paths they are treading together. The discussion may focus sharply on a given issue in one phase of the work under

---

* Quoted from a digest of Constance Warren's *A new design for women's education*, p. 2. By permission of J. B. Lippincott.

74

discussion. At other times the discussion will move down related by-paths. The instructor rarely lectures to his class or tells his students the answers. He urges them to bring in their own opinions and thresh them out in class. Students accustomed to progressive school methods move into this atmosphere easily and purposefully. Students from the conservative boarding school or the conventional college find it an exhilarating new experience.*

The remainder of the student's time is devoted to reading in connection with the course and working on an individual project related to the course.

These individual projects mean independent research in the library and in the field, occasionally paralleling the mainstream of the course itself, but often going off on a tangent. When the student has rounded up her material, drawn her conclusions, set them down in clear form, she is ready to contribute her report to the pool of group experience, provided her instructor thinks it suitable for classroom discussion. She has prepared and marshaled all the supporting evidence she can find. Now she is ready to defend her conclusions before a jury of her peers, all posted in the broad aspects of the subject at hand.†

The attendance at the weekly conference or seminar is supplemented by a weekly or biweekly individual conference with her instructor, a conference that may be devoted to a discussion of the subject matter and reading concerned or to the progress of the individual project on which each student is engaged.

It is obvious that this system, in contrast to the conventional lecture-recitation-quiz-examination system, places a heavy responsibility on the student to develop good habits of working independently, of seeking out and finding materials, and—from the beginning of her college experience

* *Ibid.*, p. 4.
† *Idem.*

—of organizing such materials into an effective narrative or argument. It is obvious, also, that this system discourages or makes impossible the dripping-on-the-sponge educational process, checks the teacher's often uncontrolled verbalism, and makes the student largely responsible for educating herself.

In order that the student, working under this free system, should learn the proper use of her powers, her energies, and her time, such experimental colleges as Sarah Lawrence and Bennington provide a great deal of guidance of individual students by individual members of the faculty. At both these colleges this advisory faculty-student relationship is regarded as an essential and significant part of the whole educational program. At Bennington certain of the more experienced members of the faculty devote as much as half their time to work of this sort, and consider this work as important as their more formal teaching. Both Sarah Lawrence and Bennington consider it of the greatest importance to discover the student's aptitudes and interests and to assist the student by the wisest counsel available in making the difficult adjustment from the dependent relationship of the family circle to the independent status of the mature and adult student.[13]

A special feature of the Bennington system is the two months' period during the winter when the college is not in session. It would be a mistake, however, to regard this period as an overextended holiday. It is instead to be considered, in the terminology of Bennington, as a "winter field period."

Plans for the most effective use of the Winter Field Period are made by each student in consultation with her counselor or tutor. The war has greatly multiplied both the need and the opportunities for voluntary work within the capacity of younger students. As students gain skills, they can secure increasingly interesting jobs; and for Senior Division students, Winter Field Period work tends to be related more closely to the student's major emphasis in College. Fourth year students generally use their last Winter Field Period to advance or complete work on their senior projects, taking advantage of library and other facilities in the metropolitan centers. The College assumes responsibility for helping the student plan her winter work, and for gathering reports about her from the agencies or people to whom she has been responsible.*

Such a device as the Winter Field Period may serve a special purpose in such an institution as Bennington in counteracting a possible tendency to make the individual studdent the object of an excessive amount of attention. Her experience in adjusting to work or study outside the college walls may very well deepen her sense of responsibility to other persons than herself and may also bring home to her a sense of the forces that check the operation of completely free and independent individual behavior.

A significant feature of the Sarah Lawrence and Bennington systems is the de-emphasization of examinations. On this point, the Bennington official announcement is pertinent:

No final comprehensive examinations are given. The student's whole accomplishment is considered in recommending her for the degree. In most majors, some important piece of individual work has been done, and its successful completion is part of the evidence of the student's competence.

At Bennington, the student's advancement from one to another stage of her course is determined, not—as in the University of Chicago system—by the number of examinations passed, nor by an accumulation of satisfactory reports in all courses, but by more fundamental considerations.

* "Announcement for the Year 1942-43," *Bennington College Bulletin*, p. 16.

Decisions as to promotion are made by a committee of the faculty on the basis of the student's total record in College; but an accumulation of satisfactory reports in all courses taken is neither necessary nor sufficient for promotion. The judgment of the committee looks to the future rather than to the past: is the student now capable of doing the sustained, independent work which in two more years will result in the kind of specialized competence and general orientation certified by the awarding of the Bennington degree? Her record may include some failures or false starts; but if she has demonstrated serious interest and good capacity, and has attained a clear sense of direction, she is promoted. If she has satisfactory standing in all courses, yet lacks the genuine interest which would make her an active and responsible partner in her own education, she is not promoted.*

Nor is graduation from Bennington dependent on the passing of final comprehensive examinations. In the absence of such examinations, it is incumbent on the faculty to determine the student's graduation on the basis of her total record and her performance in the individual project on which she has been engaged.

The work of the last two years should lead to no intense climax, marking the end of formal education and the beginning of adult life. The purposes of the College would be defeated if the degree should come to be regarded as the objective, or the terminal point, of education.†

The Sarah Lawrence view of final examinations clearly parallels that at Bennington.

In this type of education something else counts even more than what the student learns; that is, the effect which learning has upon the student. Has it added to her understanding of herself in relation to those about her and to the world in

* "Announcement for the Year 1942-43," pp. 12-13.
† *Ibid.*, p. 17.

which she lives? Has it opened her eyes to things of which she has been unaware, or which she has taken for granted? Has it started a train of thought which keeps moving? It is the answers to questions like these, always in the background of the instructor's mind as he teaches, that come to light in the running report kept of each student for the purpose of judging her growth. Formal examinations, like marks, reveal few of these psychological effects of education.*

As this passage suggests, grades in final or comprehensive examinations have given place to "the running report kept of each student for the purpose of judging her growth." This phrase hardly does justice to the extent of this "running report." Each member of the faculty is called upon to submit fairly full reports at frequent intervals, not merely of the quality and quantity of work done by a student in his course, but also of the psychological state of the student and the kind and quality of affective, emotional, intellectual interest and curiosity she is exhibiting. Each "don" also submits at frequent intervals fairly full reports on his observations of the student "donees." The result is the rapid accumulation of a very imposing amount of data on each student and her record. The significance of these reports is considered and reconsidered by a responsible faculty committee, and on the basis of their recommendations, the student is asked to leave the college or to continue her work and finally be recommended for her degree. The result of this procedure is that the college has a kind and quantity of record and report far more indicative of the rate and pace of the student's intellectual progress than is furnished by the conventional, though frequently highly complicated, system of hours-credit and grades and grade-points characteristic of most liberal arts colleges.

Anyone who has had experience of faculty meetings

* Warren, *op. cit.*, p. 2.

considering candidates for graduation in a conventional liberal arts college will be impressed by the absurdity of the hours-credit-grade-point system of determining graduation or failure to graduate. Cases arise repeatedly in which there is a deficiency in hours-credit but an excess of grade-points or an excess in hours-credit and a deficiency of grade-points. Such a system calls out the higher mathematical powers of deans and faculties, but it ignores the really fundamental problem of whether or not the student has made a sufficient amount of intellectual progress between his freshman and his senior year to justify his recommendation for a degree. There is no reason for wonder that the Pennsylvania Survey discovered a considerable number of college seniors who were less well-informed than a considerable number of high-school seniors. Yet, despite this damaging fact, most of the inferior seniors would "earn" a degree by means of the hours-credit-grade-point system.

The educational philosophy and system characteristic of such colleges as Sarah Lawrence and Bennington offer, then, the sharpest possible contrast to the conventional liberal arts system. In the light of the practice of the experimental institutions, the practice of the conventional colleges seems anachronistic, medieval, and formalistic, and the results, educationally, almost meaningless.[14]

Not only at such experimental institutions as Sarah Lawrence, Bennington, and Scripps, but at more conventional institutions like Vassar, the University of Iowa, and the University of Texas, there is a surprising amount of emphasis on teaching by the studio-method, and there is hardly a well-known liberal arts college that does not boast of the more or less permanent presence on its faculty of one or more creative artists. The motivation behind the addition of creative artists to a faculty is not always simple or clear, but the results of such additions are pedagogically significant. In many instances—especially in the case of the universities—creative or interpretive artists have seemed normal increments to the faculty in departments or schools of music or of the fine arts. In some instances, either institutions or foundations have felt that the college or the university might furnish a sympathetic atmosphere and milieu in which the creative artist might create happily. Thus, the institution takes the place of the personal patron of earlier centuries, just as for a time the United States Government took over such functions, during the depression of the thirties, in very influential and productive Federal Art Projects.

The effect of this relationship upon the creative artist is a problem not quite relevant to this investigation, but a tentative answer to the problem may nevertheless be suggested. The results vary inevitably not only with the temperament of the artist but also with the particular academic milieu in which he is attempting to function. Certain artists find the academic milieu a congenial one, and are able to go on with the work steadily and happily. Others feel, as Kurt Roesch of Sarah Lawrence says, that "though the winter may be lost, there is always the summer." Others —with perhaps less creative urge—find their energies almost entirely absorbed in teaching; in such cases, they may or may not make a contribution to the academic community more vital and more significant than that of the non-creative teacher. Unless they do make a more significant contribution and unless they are able to keep on with their own creative work, their connection with an academic institution may be difficult to justify. The effect of the academic environment on the artist again depends on the character of that environment. Certain administrators and department heads who give lip-service to the notion that it is a good thing to have artists in the academic community make it practically impossible for them to do any creative work by giving them a full-time teaching-load. There are probably relatively few instances in which the creative activity of the artist is regarded as a legitimate part of the artist's teaching-load. Artists who find themselves in such rarely encountered circumstances are indeed to be envied.

From the point of view of the student—who, pedagogically at least, is the element that deserves primary consideration—the particular contribution of the artist differs markedly from that of the conventional academic teacher. He is concerned primarily with creating; the academic teacher is concerned either with a systematic historical study of what has been created or an intensive analytical study of what has been created. The artist has a special inside view of the motivation and the technique of the creative process. He may be a very bad historian or a very unsystematic esthetician, but, if he is genuinely creative, he is interested above all in adding his mite to the world's store of created values embodied in works of art. His *locus operandi* is not the classroom but the studio; his materials are those of the special medium in which he works; his subject matter is decided, not by historical or philosophical considerations, but by his own temperamental inclination and preoccupation.

What the artist does contribute to the methodology of liberal arts education differs fundamentally, however, from what he contributes to the methodology of education in a professional art school. If he understands properly his relation to the liberal arts education, he will realize that he is legitimately concerned, not with training professional artists but with training cultivated patrons of the arts. His aim, therefore, must not be the discovery and the promotion of individual talents, although some such activity may be unavoidable. His aim is the initiation of as many students as possible into some understanding of the potentialities and the limitations of the various media in which artists work. His aim may very sensibly be that of the artists on the faculty of Scripps College, who, according to the sculptor Albert Stewart, set nonproduction as their goal. That is to say, they are not concerned with the number of works of art—amateurish or semiprofessional—produced by students; they are rather concerned with giving students some limited experience of the actual creative process.

The value of such experience of the actual creative process seems uncontestable. For it is a kind of experience in the fine arts, music, or literature which no other type of discipline can give. It makes the student aware of the difficulties to be faced and the skills to be achieved if the work produced is to come anywhere near approximating the vision with which the artist was first stirred. It encourages a kind of activity and brings out—if only to a limited degree—powers of which the student may have been completely unaware, and which no other type of discipline is adapted to bring out. The view expressed by D. M. Mendelowitz of Stanford University that every student in the field of the humanities should have some slight practical experience in some one of the fine arts, in music, or in imaginative writing is one that ought to commend itself to increasing numbers of college educators.

The most recent successful attempt to restore the esthetic approach to works of art to its position of legitimate primacy and to assign to properly subordinate positions the historical, psychological, and ethical approaches is the contemporary movement in pedagogy and criticism to which I assign the title, "The return to the text." The aim and the methods involved in the return to the text are suggestively stated in the description of the Bennington College course in Literature and the Humanities: "The primary aim is to help the student make an adequate response

83

to some of the more important forms of verbal expression that have emerged in Western culture. Emphasis is on training of the intelligence and sensibility through discussion and intensive analysis of a few selected texts. Extensive use is made of reading aloud; there are frequent practical exercises in both expository and imaginative writing, and numerous concrete problems of interpretation. The method entails consideration of all the relevant aspects —moral, esthetic, sociological—of each of the works under study." * The return to the text is perhaps the most promising innovation in contemporary teaching techniques, since it can be adopted without any modification of program and without additional expenditures for personal and for objective paraphernalia.

There are four major modes of approaching works of art: historical, psychological, ethical, and esthetic. Of these, the historical is the one in which most college and university teachers have been trained, and the one which, accordingly, they most steadily emphasize. The literary historian studies the work of art in relation to the personality of the artist, as a means of understanding the life and thought of the historical period in which the work was produced, or as an entity in the realm of man-made things, a product of man's manual and technical adroitness and skill.† The psychological mode of attack regards the work of art as a means of satisfying, symbolically, the complex pattern of the individual's "appetencies" and "revulsions," to use I. A. Richards' suggestive terms, and as a medium leading to the psychological extension or intensification of the individual's sensory or imaginative experience.

* "Announcement for the Year, 1942-1943," *Bennington College Bulletin*, Vol. 10, No. 4, p. 22.
† This last type of historical study concerns the physical aspects of a manuscript or book or painting or piece of sculpture rather than the esthetic or moral or intellectual aspects.

The ethical mode of approach concerns itself with the doctrine or dogma explicit in the work of art; with the fidelity with which the work represents life; the illumination with which it interprets it; and the cogency with which it illustrates, or tends to demonstrate the validity of, some philosophical, economic, political, social, or religious dogma. The esthetic approach to a work of art is concerned with the effectiveness of the work of art as a work of art or with its effectiveness relative to the class to which it belongs. The two fundamental processes in the esthetic mode of attack are those of comprehension (or interpretation, in a strict sense of the word) and of evaluation. The esthetic attack ignores biographical * and historical considerations and keeps ethical and philosophical considerations in the subordinate position in which they belong. It assumes that a work of art is not merely form or structure or texture but an experience, an experience of the artist's representation and interpretation of his real or imagined world, an experience the value of which—emotional, moral, intellectual—can be decided only after the closest critical analysis of form or structure or texture.

An abundance of evidence has accumulated to support the contention that the return to literary texts is not only an eminently desirable but an extremely exacting procedure. At the end of Goethe's life, he said to Eckermann, "These good people do not know how much time and effort it takes to learn how to read. I have been working at it for eighty years and I cannot say that I have succeeded yet." † In recent years there have been repeated expressions of the

* "The comprehension of a work of art is, actually, seldom impaired by a lack of biographical knowledge." René Wellek, "Literary History," in *Literary scholarship, its aims and methods*, by Norman Foerster, *et al.* (The University of North Carolina Press, 1941), p. 102.

† Quoted by Gilbert Chinard, "Literature and the Humanities," in *The meaning of the humanities* (Princeton University Press, 1938), p. 156.

view Goethe held. In a lively attack on pseudo-scholarship, the distinguished English novelist, E. M. Forster, wrote: "Books have to be read (worse luck, for it takes a long time); it is the only way of discovering what they contain. A few savage tribes eat them, but reading is the only method of assimilation revealed to the west. The reader must sit down alone and struggle with the writer, and this the pseudo-scholar will not do. He would rather relate a book to the history of its time, to events in the life of its author, to the events it describes, above all to some tendency. As soon as he can use the word 'tendency' his spirits rise, and though those of his audience may sink, they often pull out their pencils at this point, and make a note, under the impression that a tendency is portable." * (It is significant that what Forster attacks as pseudo-scholarship is regarded in America as serious scholarship.) More recently, Clifton Fadiman in his account of his career as reader and critic, "My Life is an Open Book," has added his testimony on this point. "Serious reading is an art. An art is something you have to learn. To learn an art requires a teacher. There are too few teachers of reading in the United States, and that is one of the reasons why we are still only a semi-educated people. I, like my fellow Americans, was never taught, in elementary and high school, how to read properly." He goes on to say that the man who taught him to read was John Erskine, and he ascribes Erskine's remarkable success as a teacher of reading to the fact that he had "enormous respect (not merely liking) for his subject matter," and, in addition, he challenged his students to understand what they were reading. He called upon them "for a kind of mental exercise that is ordinarily devoted to mastering such 'hard' subjects as philosophy and the sciences." †

* E. M. Forster, *Aspects of the novel* (Harcourt, Brace, 1927), p. 28.
† Clifton Fadiman, *Reading I've liked* (Simon and Schuster, 1942), pp. xxix-xxx.

Finally, the inexhaustible character of the reading process is made clear by René Wellek's observation that "The work of art is an objective construct whose full meaning cannot be exhausted by generations of readers." [15]

It is not without significance that two critics as far apart in time and in theory as Hazlitt and Eliot should agree on the need for the closest kind of textual analysis. In Hazlitt's essay, "On criticism," he wrote, criticism at first "is generally satisfied to give an opinion whether a work is good or bad, and to quote a passage or two in support of this opinion; afterwards, it is bound to assign the reasons of its decision and to analyze supposed beauties or defects with *microscopic minuteness*." * And Eliot, as recently as 1933, affirmed his belief in the importance of "that minute and scrupulous examination of felicity and blemish, line by line, which is conspicuously absent from the criticism of our time," and went on to express the wish that "we might dispose more attention to the correctness of expression, to the clarity or obscurity, to the grammatical precision or inaccuracy, to the choice of words, whether just or improper, exalted or vulgar, of our verse." † In the light of these admonitions, we are encouraged to maintain that no poetic text can be said to have been read until its theme has been discovered, the tones with which the poet has invested it have been analyzed, the ethical and philosophical implications elucidated, the nature of the structure established, and the contributions measured of the structure, the technical point of view, the diction, sound pattern, imagery, figures of speech, and metrics to the total effectiveness of the poem. Similarly, no piece of fiction has been read on every esthetic level, until its theme, tone,

* William Hazlitt, *Table talk, or original essays*, Everyman's Library (London: J. M. Dent and Co., 1908), p. 214. Italics mine.

† T. S. Eliot, *The use of poetry and the use of criticism* (Harvard University Press, 1933), pp. 15-16.

ethical and philosophical implications, structure, characteristics, and style have been analyzed and synthesized.

It is too early in the development of the return-to-the-
text movement to write its history, but it is not too early to
indicate some of the forces that lie behind this development. Since I am more familiar with the development of
the "back-to-the-text" movement in literature than in the
fine arts, history, or philosophy, I may perhaps be permitted to consider especially the forces operative upon this innovation in the teaching of literature.

The most powerful initial influence was the publication
of I. A. Richards' *Practical criticism* in 1929. Richards had
already attracted wide attention by his theories of the nature of the esthetic experience and its complexities in his
Principles of literary criticism (1924), but the later volume
had, if not a greater influence, a closer pertinence to problems involved in the teaching of literature. What that volume demonstrated beyond question was that the art of
reading is a very difficult art, and that there are a number
of distinctly distinguishable obstacles in the way of achieving true readings. Richards' points were driven home by
the exhibition of an accumulation of horrors in the form of
misreadings by English university undergraduates of poems
of no very great difficulty.* The book made it painfully
clear that very few undergraduates had been properly
trained in handling the most elementary features of poetic
technique. It gave rise to a resolve on the part of many
teachers to turn their attention to the problem of the development of techniques that would train students to be good
readers.

A more limited influence may be assigned to the work

* Incidentally, this collection of horrors goes far to destroy the myth
of the immense superiority of English university education to American
university education. Illiteracy seems quite as common on one side of
the Atlantic as on the other.

done by Professor Edith Rickert and her students on the graphic analysis of imagery, words, thought patterns, rhythms, and tone patterns, a technique set forth in her *New methods for the study of literature* (The University of Chicago Press, 1927). It is of interest to note the comments on her method made by Allen Tate. Tate pointed out that "Miss Rickert has constructed two schemes by means of which the elements of a piece of writing may be mathematically exhibited: statistical tabulation . . . and graphical representation, where the curves stand for the amount of use to which a literary effect is put in the progress of a given work." Tate felt that Miss Rickert's method was of little assistance in the qualitative problems of criticism, because it did not "permit the critic to know a good style from a bad" one, or "yield to the contemporary writer a useful set of instruments and directions. . . . Dreiser and James may appear numerically different in the graph; the difference in quality cannot be summed and put into the record. Yet it is with problems of quality that criticism, as distinguished from pedagogy, must always be primarily occupied." Despite his very important reservations, however, Tate concluded that Miss Rickert's method "has, nevertheless, a singular virtue, and if the teachers who may use it can be counted on for a critical application of its devices, it will tend to lift the teaching of a fine art out of the current muddle of moral exhortation and propaganda. *It concentrates on the properties of literature as art.*" *

* *The New Republic*, April 27, 1927, pp. 281-82. The italics are mine. Another influence making for the development of a movement back to the text is that of the French *explication de textes*. A close study would be required to determine the avenues through which this method has reached American educators and the extent to which its influence is operative. The French method of explication has great values in training students in the closest kind of reading and in sensitizing them to the greatest refinements of style. In unskilled or uninspired hands, it can be even more deadly than the haphazard methods of most American

Richards has, however, had a far greater influence than Miss Rickert on critics who happen to be teachers and on those who are not. To trace his influence on criticism is beyond the scope of this survey, and indeed to attribute to this single influence the rise of a distinguished school of critics who read more closely than any critics in the past have done would be historically unsound. There is more than one cause for the renascence of criticism in America in the period since the First World War.[16] An influence that aids and abets that of Richards is that of John Crowe Ransom, a kind of unofficial dean of the group of Southern writers, most of whom have at one time or another been connected with Vanderbilt University, and some of whom were the leading figures in the Fugitive group. Though Richards tends perhaps to overemphasize the psychological values of literature, and Ransom the purely esthetic values, they are at one in their encouragement of the closest kind of reading as applied to specific literary works.[17]

But the influences of Richards and Ransom are not the sole agencies that have turned the attention of teachers and students to the closest sort of scrutiny of specific texts. The elevation of Robert Maynard Hutchins to the presidency of the University of Chicago led in due time to the enunciation of his educational philosophy in various lectures and addresses, but especially in the volumes *The higher learning in America* (Yale University Press, 1936) and *No friendly voice* (The University of Chicago Press, 1936). Without presenting the arguments that led to President Hutchins' conclusion, we may cite as pertinent in this connection his view that the basic studies in the American curriculum should be

teaching of the humanities. In general, perhaps, it tends to err in an overemphasis on the merely stylistic aspects of works of art. It may be true, as the French say, that the style is the man, but the work of art, like a man, is something more than a style.

those books which have through the centuries attained to the dimensions of classics. Many such books, I am afraid, are in the ancient and medieval period. But even these are contemporary. A classic is a book that is contemporary in any age. . . . Such books are then a part, and a large part, of the permanent studies. They are so in the first place because they are the best books we know. . . . In the second place these books are an essential part of general education because it is impossible to understand any subject and to comprehend the contemporary world without them.[18]

President Hutchins' support of the "great books" theory involved, of course, his conviction that the foundation of education must ultimately be philosophy and that there should be a revival of the medieval arts of grammar, rhetoric, and logic.[19] But his advocacy of the "great books" theory has won a wider acceptance than his other educational doctrines, and has made its distinct contribution, not only at the University of Chicago but elsewhere, to the movement back to the text.[20]

At the University of Chicago, the department whose program and procedures show the deepest influence of President Hutchins' views is the Department of English under the chairmanship of Ronald S. Crane. The objectives of the Department are set forth in the pamphlet entitled *Requirements for degrees in English:*

. . . For the student of English the essential disciplines, as determined by the kinds of books and problems with which he has to deal, are four in number: (1) literary criticism, or the principles of analysis useful for the understanding and appreciation of imaginative works; (2) the analysis of ideas, or the principles applicable to the reading and judgment of writings of a theoretical or rhetorical type; (3) history, or the principles involved in the construction of good historical demonstrations and narratives; and (4) linguistics, or the principles involved in any systematic approach to the problems of language.[21]

91

The distinction of the Chicago program lies, not only in the clarity with which the objectives of undergraduate training are distinguished and defined but—more significantly—in the emphasis on the confrontation of the work of art or the work of thought by the student and—most significantly—in the training of the student in the approaches appropriate to these various works. It seems doubtful if any other contemporary undergraduate program in the humanities would show the breadth and balance of the Chicago program or a similar de-emphasization of the historical approach to literature and emphasis on the critical and analytical approaches.*

Although the major influences that motivated the movement back to the text are those indicated above, a more searching study of influences would perhaps show other significant forces, not only within the field of literature but also in allied artistic fields. For the return to the text is not merely a literary movement; indeed, its significance would be far less great if it were not paralleled by similar movements in the field of music and the fine arts. There is abundant evidence of the development of a reaction from the purely historical approach to music and the fine arts in favor of a critical and analytical approach to them. Since the development has not been quite simultaneous, the interaction of one phase of the movement upon another is more complex than can be described or illustrated here. There may, however, be some point in raising the question

* In the course of my preparation of this survey, I made it a point to "interview" University of Chicago students who were completing or had completed their training under this program, and I was repeatedly impressed by the students' understanding of the objectives and the methods that they were experiencing. I doubt very much whether undergraduates in most other institutions would manifest anything like the same clarity as to the intentions and procedures to which they were submitting.

as to which of the humanities have been the more easily accessible to the development of the movement away from the historical approach in the direction of an analytical attack upon the text itself.

I should hazard the suggestion that history and music were perhaps the humanities subjects which first manifested the tendency under discussion. In the field of history, the tendency expressed itself in a reaction from the study of modern textbooks on ancient or medieval or modern history to the study and analysis of the primary sources of historical information. Such a collection as James Harvey Robinson's *Readings in European History* (1906) was a pioneer in this movement, and it was followed by numerous imitators. As a result of this process, undergraduates majoring in history are now clearly conscious of the distinction between primary and secondary sources, and in the hands of good teachers develop some skill in the manipulation and evaluation of such sources.*

Because of the very nature of music, the study of music has been protected from the worst excesses of the merely historical approach and has been hospitable to the development of analytical techniques. Its abstract and intangible qualities have preserved it from some of the damage wrought on the visual arts and literature by an extreme preoccupation with the historical method. The visual arts and literature tempt the historian to treat the materials they offer as documents for historical manipulation; similarly, they tempt the critic to create verbal substitutes for the works that in some cases may prove valuable in themselves, but that in the last analysis are only substitute-

* Professor F. G. Marcham of Cornell has been working for a period of years on the development of materials and methods by which students from the sixth grade on can be trained in the handling of primary historical source-material. These materials and methods have been tested repeatedly in the public schools of Iowa, and they are presently to be made available for general use.

93

works and are at best descriptive and not analytical. The description of music leads to such obviously unsound and indefensible results that students of this art have drawn back from its absurdities and have tended to develop techniques for the close analysis of specific musical compositions. The development of these techniques has been immeasurably hastened by the invention and improvement of mechanical devices for reproducing music; in consequence, there is perhaps no more striking event in contemporary humanistic pedagogy than the wide use and influence of records in connection with music study.

The results of this procedure in the classroom are less exciting and suggestive than the results of the informal and more or less uninstructed education the young have achieved for themselves through the collection of musical records and through the extension of their acquaintance with musical masterpieces as presented over the radio. My first experience with a mechanism for reproducing music was with a music box that played records made of perforated steel disks. My second experience was with the perforated paper records devised for "player-pianos." The orientation of contemporary students in the field of music —as compared to students in the period before the First World War—is clearly due to no influence so much as the incredible improvement in mechanical devices for reproducing music and for sending music over the air-waves. It is further significant that this increased orientation has been very largely self-motivated and self-directed, although even the elementary schools today give their pupils a far more adequate initiation in music than did the elementary schools of the nineties.

Numerous examples could be cited of introductory analytical courses now available in the more progressive schools and universities, but two or three illustrations must suffice. At Bennington College, for example, the intention of the introductory course, The Language of Music, is "to approach the medium of music as a whole through the study of vocal music. Emphasis is mainly on the elementary language of music—rhythm and meter, tempo, dynamics, intervals and scales, and three-part harmony." In addition, students are introduced to "the basic forms in musical literature from the medieval to the contemporary, although the order is not chronological . . . Instrumental forms and more complex works in the vocal forms are studied through the use of phonograph records . . . Records are analyzed outside of class to develop the student's listening power." The following course, Main Developments in Western Music, is a continuation of the introductory course, "except for a gradual shifting to more complex specimens of the literature in the instrumental as well as the vocal forms." * At Vassar, the introductory course, Music as a Literature, which surveys the chief trends in the development of music, from the stylistic and esthetic standpoints, is followed by advanced courses, Analysis of Design (the principles of design in music; homophonic and polyphonic form in the classic and romantic styles) and Analysis of Texture (basic harmonic effects and their various textural elaborations in the classic, romantic, and post-romantic styles), and by specialized analytical courses in the symphony, chamber music, and the opera. At the University of California, the Introduction to Musical Literature consists of "lectures, illustrations, and readings designed to furnish a general appreciation of music." The course is limited to 575 students, and on two occasions when it has been given, three hundred students who have applied for the course have had to be refused because it was impossible to accommodate them.

* "Announcement for the Year 1942-43," *Bennington College Bulletin*, p. 24.

95

Weekly section meetings are devoted to "listening, discussions, and written work." *

The fine arts have been somewhat tardy in their introduction of analytical methods, and have been too long addicted to the communication of merely historical information. Everyone is familiar with the deadening and deadly procedures in conventional courses in the history of art, the overemphasis on recognition and identification, the memorization of slides, and the testing of the student on information about the author, the name of the work, its location, and its esthetic category. All too frequently such training failed to give the student any guidance in his own behavior in the presence of an unfamiliar and particular work of art. A good student might be trained to recognize, as Hallie Flanagan says satirically, that "the brush-work belongs to the artist's third period," but he was quite unprepared for independent and accurate analysis of either a familiar or an unfamiliar work of art, and had received little or no guidance in the principles governing the evaluation of works of art.

But there is a tide even in the teaching of the fine arts, and there is good reason to believe that the tide has turned. An excellent example of the results of this turning of the tide is such a course as the Analysis of Visual Art, which is now one of the Basic Studies in the curriculum of Bennington College. "The purpose of the course is to develop perception and understanding of visual art, and secondarily, to present a grammar of visual art by means of which the student may be able to recognize for herself the principles involved in the creation and appreciation of significant works. By means of such initial definition the student learns also to understand more clearly the terms used in any discussion of the visual arts as a whole. Basic principles are

* "General Catalog, 1941-42," *University of California Bulletin*, p. 342.

approached through practical exercises in pure design, requiring the use of line, texture, and tone (colors, value, and intensity) in two- and three-dimensional compositions. They are further recognized and made part of the student's visual language through the analysis of a selected number of works of art both ancient and modern, abstract and representational." * But Bennington is not alone in its initiation of analytical introductory courses in the analysis of pictorial and plastic works of art. At the University of Chicago, a course in The Criticism of Works of Art furnishes an introduction to practical art criticism through the discussion of "selected works of art, with emphasis on method and procedure and on the general principles of the fine arts." † At the University of Iowa, a course in Art Criticism is devoted to a study of esthetic theory and its application to the practical criticism of the visual arts. Students in this course are trained in finding "bases of constructive art criticism through a study of the nature of beauty, theory of art, and history of taste." Such problems are discussed as "the part which taste plays in criticism, the importance of form and of content in the art object, art for art's sake versus art for propaganda, and the relations between art and beauty, art and religion, art and industrial design, and art and the social structure." ‡ These examples may suffice to indicate the parallel development in the teaching of the fine arts of the tendency to supplement the purely historical study of the arts with the more basic and essential analytical and esthetic study.

As in the field of music, this tendency has been hastened by the vast improvement in techniques for reproducing

* "Announcement for the Year 1942-43," *Bennington College Bulletin*, p. 25.
† "The Summer Quarter, 1942," *The University of Chicago Announcements*, p. 57.
‡ "Summer Session Catalogue Number, 1942," *University of Iowa Publication*, pp. 6-7.

works of art. The ludicrous inadequacy of earlier reproductions may be suggested by reminding the more mature reader of the "Perry Pictures" that were popular classroom auxiliaries in elementary schools in the nineties. No improvement has been more striking than that in the field of color-reproduction. The embarkation of museums like the Museum of Modern Art on an elaborate program of publication of illustrated catalogues makes possible an orientation of the contemporary student somewhat similar to his orientation by means of musical recordings and radio performances. It is probably indicative of the highly verbal character of teachers of literature and of their consequent distaste for mechanisms and gadgets that, in the main, they have made slight use of such mechanisms in the teaching of literature. There now exist, thanks to the activity primarily of English and Continental agencies, a large library of recordings of literary works made by authors or by professional readers, actors, and actresses. Certainly this material is not used to nearly the extent that is obviously desirable. In consequence, most teachers and students are eye-readers and not ear-readers. A wider use of literary recordings in the classroom would sharpen the ears of both teachers and students, and would give both groups a kind of direct, if unanalyzed, experience of the literary work from which they willfully cut themselves off by confining themselves to eye-reading, which is almost always utterly superficial and inattentive, particularly because the inundation of the modern teacher and student by printed matter of all grades of worth has forced superficial reading habits upon them.

In my estimation, no development in pedagogical methods holds the promise for the humanities of the movement-back-to-the-text.[22] Its advantages over other experimental pedagogical techniques are its inexpensiveness and its freedom from any complexity of administrative organization or program. American higher education has been prone to overlook the fact that no educational system is better than the men who operate it, and to look for new types of programs or new administrative procedures as panaceas by means of which to escape the inadequacies of our methods and our disappointment in their results. The back-to-the-text movement is a procedure that does not require elaborate or expensive administrative apparatus or extensive personnel. All it requires is a teacher and a student, a text, and a meeting place for the three. A further asset of the technique is that it is applicable at any stage of the educational program. It will be objected by teachers habituated to traditional procedures that the techniques of intensive analysis are inappropriate and inaccessible to any but the best undergraduates. It is true that on every succeeding level of education a greater subtlety and maturity ought to be demanded of students trained in this method, but the method can be adapted to the earliest stages of the student's experience of works of art and even the most naive or the most insensitive student can gain much from it. In my experience, the accomplishments of high-grade freshmen have been demonstrably superior to those of upperclassmen untrained in such techniques.

The back-to-the-text movement is perhaps the surest weapon available in the eternal war against pedants, irresponsible esthetes, and professional scholars. Its quintessential value is that it brings the student into immediate and intimate contact with particular works of art and trains him in the kind of behavior appropriate to a perceptive and cultivated person in that situation. It is the clearest road to the kinds of value in which the humanities are particularly rich, the values of discrimination and judgment, of fidelity to the fact, and of the deeper and richer values of which the arts are the repository—the values of beauty, goodness, and truth.

99

CHAPTER IV

PERSONNEL IN THE HUMANITIES

ANY consideration of personnel in the humanities may very well take its point of departure from the recent socio-logical study of the academic profession, Logan Wilson's *The academic man.** The profile drawn by Professor Wilson is that of a person usually of lower middle-class origin, who has passed through a prolonged and highly formalized training—high school, college or university, and graduate school—and who works himself up, financially, professionally, and, to a slighter degree, socially, through a complicated system of promotions that result from his devotion to the activities demanded or expected of him: teaching, committee work, research, and publication.[1] Many of the stigmata of the academic profession are accounted for by the socioeconomic origin of a large majority of its members and by the nature of their training. Although in some circles, the college professor is supposed to harbor various subversive social and political doctrines, "his political and social views seldom go beyond the preconceptions of the middle class to which he belongs." †

Professionally, the academic man is concerned with attaining a status, characterized by stability—the technical term is "tenure"—and prestige. The stability increases as the ambitious or socially and economically insecure young academician mounts the scale from assistant to instructor,

---

* Logan Wilson, *The academic man, a study in the sociology of a profession,* 1942. By permission of Oxford University Press, New York.
† *Ibid.,* p. 117.

from assistant professor to "full" professor. His prestige depends on a number of complex factors: the favor with which he is regarded by his colleagues, within and outside the institution to which he is attached, and, more significantly, by the administrative officers—head of department, dean, and college or university president—in whose hands his undramatic fate lies. The esteem in which he is held depends, in varying degrees in various institutions, on his virtues and defects as a human being, the virtues and defects of his wife, his willingness to serve on important and unimportant committees, the number of inches covered by a printed bibliography of his publications, and, last and frequently least, his success as a teacher and his knowledge of his subject. The state of being a "full" professor is the far-off divine event in the academician's existence.

Of the characteristics of the academic group generally, Professor Wilson writes:

Since graduate work is from the economic point of view a more accessible channel for vertical mobility than are most other types of professional training, it is logical to assume (but difficult to prove) that mental superiority is more often coupled with proletarian characteristics among scientists and scholars than is the case in other professions. It appears, then, that individual instances of faulty speech, boorish manners, bad dress, and general uncouthness are primarily the results of a system of selection that stresses what a man knows rather than how he appears.*

This is a harsh indictment, but it is not without justice. The social background of the academic man and the highly specialized character of his training are hindrances rather than helps in creating a wide range of cultural interests or a devotion to values—at least in terms of a scale of living—that are less materialistic and gadget-minded than those of

* *Ibid.*, p. 20.

the American civilization of which the professor is a humble part.

The somewhat unlovely profile drawn by Professor Wilson needs to be softened by at least two considerations the writer has ignored: first, the very real satisfactions—some of them petty and ignoble, others legitimate and admirable—which the academic life offers its practitioners, and, second, the unselfish, altruistic aspects of professional activity.[2]

The academic man shares with other Americans the habits of sympathy for need and suffering and of generous responsiveness to such sympathy. Without making invidious comparisons with other nations, it is notorious that Americans respond with unparalleled generosity to appeals made anywhere in the world for relief from natural or social disasters. This generosity is peculiarly conspicuous in the academic man; in fact, he is probably the easiest "pushover" for legitimate and illegitimate philanthropic appeals. Despite the pressures that lead him and his family to approximate the living standards of the "upper middle" or "lower upper" stratum of society, he is perhaps the least money-minded of the professional class. The reasons for this freedom from money-mindedness are complex. One of the reasons is his conscious choice of a career in which the financial rewards are notoriously slight in comparison to those of business, industry, and some of the other professions. It is commonly charged—or at least thought—by hard-headed business men that a college professor *is* a college professor because he knows—at least subconsciously—that he would be a failure at anything else. This is the sort of charge that can be neither proved nor disproved. It is quite as reasonable to believe that the college professor is a college professor, not because he is afraid of the rough and tumble, the brutal competitiveness of the world of business, but because the values implicit in a life devoted to business seem to him dull and boring and the motivation of a career in business indefensibly self-centered. A man chooses, or is chosen for, an academic career because of a temperamental aptitude for life and work in a college community, because he likes the freedom from time clocks and from the monotony of desk work, because he prefers the kinds of employers the academic world offers him to those in the world of business and industry, because he thinks he will enjoy academic working-hours and vacation-hours, or because the academic ladder offers him the most attractive means of modest social and financial advancement. But the basic motivation—however it may be weakened by training and experience—is his interest in the kinds of knowledge and wisdom offered him by books, laboratories, and professors, and his desire to spend his life in the acquisition of such knowledge, in the sharing of it with students, and, in some cases, in pushing back the boundaries of ignorance and prejudice. This devotion to learning and to teaching may be checked by the pressure of many forces: by the deadening nature of his graduate training, by his exploitation by an unscrupulous and penny-pinching administration, by the complacent and self-indulgent academic climate in which he must live and breathe, by pressures to manifest his devotion to learning in ways essentially incongenial to his temperament, by the desiccating influence of an unimaginative and incurious routine, or by a sheer failure of mental or physical vitality. But the college professor, like the clergyman, is one of the most potent symbols in our Western pattern of culture of a devotion to values that, if not other-worldly, are intellectual and spiritual and altruistic.*

* I am unaware of any study indicating the relative incidence of neuroses in the academic profession in comparison with their incidence in other professions. It is my impression, however, that among academic men—and women—the incidence of neuroses is relatively high. Among

The members of a faculty devoting themselves to one or another subject in the field of the humanities constitute a recognizable species of the *genus academicus*. Inevitably, they are both like and unlike the other species subsumed under this genus. They have in the main the same ambitions; they are conditioned by the same socioeconomic factors; they have the same hurdles to surmount and the same laurels to which to aspire. On the whole perhaps, men in the humanities are likely to manifest a greater resistance to specialization and a wider range of purely cultural interests. They can communicate with a fair amount of ease with their colleagues in the social sciences, and some of them have been known to exchange civil words with biological and physical scientists. They are likely to be more widely oriented in literature and the fine arts, although it would be risky to count on the extracurricular taste in literature and music of even the most learned professor in the humanities. In the field of literature, many professors are inclined to take the view that literature ended with the period in which they have specialized and that nothing produced since is worthy of their attention. Toward the writers of their own period, their attitude arises from a combination of elements: ignorance, fear, and contempt.

the naive, such an assertion, if true, may seem a damaging admission. To the more sophisticated, it may very well account for many of the admirable achievements—in and out of the classroom—of the academic type. For, as the psychologists have shown us, what is important about a neurosis is not the neurosis but what one does with it. The academic man may very well prove, on close study, to be a type that is unusually skilled in turning his neurotic liabilities into assets. For the professor, a lecture may be—in Kenneth Burke's terms—a "symbolic act," a kind of strategy designed to throw off the burden of his neurosis, to dramatize it and objectify it, and to make it personally endurable and socially intelligible. Possibly the verbalism of the academic type and his frequent approximation to the "theatrical" or "prima donna" temperament may have roots in his fairly common addiction to neuroses. For subtle illustrations of the ways in which the creative artist turns his neurotic liabilities into assets, see Kenneth Burke's *The philosophy of literary form* (Louisiana State University Press, 1941) and Edmund Wilson's *The wound and the bow* (Houghton Mifflin, 1941).

Even when they lower themselves to treat contemporary literature in the classroom, they regard as contemporary the literature of their flourishing youth and not the literature contemporary with their students.

Academicians in the field of the humanities may be distinguished, not merely in terms of their departmental allegiances but by their temperamental preoccupations and aptitudes. A simple and possibly suggestive classification on this second scale is as scholars, esthetes, and teachers. The scholar is characterized by his preoccupation with research and the methods of research, with the accumulation of material and its systematic presentation with serried footnotes and with bibliographies listing his authorities. At his best, he is moved by one of the noblest of motives—the passion for extending the bounds of knowledge; at his worst, he is a pedant, immersed in minutiae, hopelessly lost in the eternal process of collecting and arranging material, and progressively incapable of putting his accumulated material to any significant use. A variation on the scholarly type in the field of the humanities is the scientific linguist, who treats words as though they were the scattered bones of some prehistoric animal and is utterly impotent of the godlike function of breathing life into those bones and making them live. The linguist is beautifully adapted, by temperament and preoccupation, to his place in the lowest circle of the academic inferno.

At the opposite end of the scale of humanistic types is the esthetic group—the pure esthete, the artist *manqué*, and the true artist. Of the members of this group, the first —the esthete—is the more common. He is the individual with the temperament but without the creative power of the genuine artist. He is much more likely than the genuine artist to call attention to his estheticism by eccentricities of dress or manner that strike his nonesthetic colleagues as "affected" but that are actually natural expressions of his taste and temperament. His characteristic response to life and the arts is not scholarly or scientific or philosophical but esthetic. Whether his taste be good or bad, he is likely to manifest widely ranging interests in the arts generally and to attempt in his teaching to impart something of his own enthusiasm for his mistress, Beauty, to the more sensitive members of his student-audience. Though he may be intellectually shallow, unrigorously critical, and too easily appreciative, he frequently furnishes his department a valuable corrective to the scholarly and historical preoccupations of his colleagues. He, at least, never loses sight of the important consideration that the humanities are, or ought to be, primarily "value-subjects," and that the practitioner who is faithful to them must ever be concerned with the elucidation, revelation, and communication of values.

A close approximation to the esthete is the artist *manqué*. The chief difference between them is that the former is usually untroubled by an urge to creative work and the latter not only has it but is troubled, if not tormented, by it. He is a man who would be an imaginative writer, musician, painter, or sculptor if he had been endowed with a little more creative drive and a good deal more creative imagination. The esthete is happy in his uncreative estheticism; the artist *manqué* bears the burden of permanent frustration. He circumvents the burden least successfully when he goes on—while youth and hope last— writing unpublishable novels or painting ignominiously bad or at least not quite good paintings. He circumvents his burden most successfully perhaps when he devotes his insight and imagination and understanding of the process of successful artistic fruition to the work of criticism. In this field—if he is not biased and embittered by his own lack of success—he may achieve not only an *Ersatz*-creation but a genuine creation, for in the eyes of time high-minded and scrupulous criticism is only slightly less important and meaningful than the work of creation.

The genuine artist is perhaps the most easily distinguishable of the three esthetic types. He may manifest few or no external stigmata of the esthetic temperament; he may look and talk like an insurance salesman; he may be conspicuously inexpressive or incessantly voluble. The only essential among the differentia is his creativeness. The only sure basis of his recognition is his work, and when his productivity ends—for external or subjective reasons—he is, in the strict meaning of the term, no longer an artist.

Of these three esthetic types, the one that is most likely to be the most gifted in teaching is the esthete. He is not distracted, as the artist *manqué* is, by the creative itch, nor is he seized, as the true artist is, by the compulsion to create, no matter what the opposing circumstances. As an acolyte or high priest of Art, he can render his most effective service to her by making converts to her, by snatching brands from the consuming fires of unawareness and insensitivity, of ignorance and provincialism. In the field of English, particularly, and possibly in the fine arts generally, the artist *manqué* is perhaps most effective pedagogically in teaching the practical elements in the arts, whether writing or painting or musical composition. The effectiveness of the true artist as teacher is by no means dependent on his productivity or the quality of his productivity as an artist. Of the skills and processes that make his artistic productions distinguished he may be unaware or at least incapable of expression and communication. The artist's chief contribution to the academic community—and it is an extremely important one—is the example given by his presence of the actual contemporary creative process, of the absorption of an adult and gifted personality in the process of creation, of the fact—obvious but frequently ignored by academic historians and scholars—that the arts did not come to an end in 1500, 1800, or even 1914, but that their creation goes on, in fair weather and foul, significantly or insignificantly. The artist in the academic community is the most conspicuous symbol of the endlessness of the living process of artistic creation, a challenging witness to the fact that art is a way of making and a medium of vision and insight and wisdom, and not merely subject matter for historical and scientific scrutiny, or defenseless material to be used in the manufacture of theses and scholarly articles.

To be distinguished alike from the scholarly and the artistic types is the "born" teacher, the person who flourishes only in his relations with students in and out of the classroom, who expresses himself most potently in his devotion to the fine art of teaching, who, at his best, achieves something of the artist's creativeness in his skill in bringing about a vital relationship between the student and what the student is learning or being taught.[3] If the esthete is marked by some of the characteristics of the artist, the "born" teacher is distinguished by some of the characteristics of the actor on the one hand, and the preacher on the other. Like the actor, he is gifted in platform skills; his personality is so plastic that it is possible for him to achieve a temporary and more or less perfect identification of himself with the subject or person that he is discussing. He handles his voice effectively; he may even become famous—as "Copey" of Harvard did—as a public reader. He is sensitive to the reactions of his audience, knows how to play upon them, is able to make effective patterns and juxtapositions of the personalities in his audience-group. Like the actor, he has a sense of timing, a flair for the effective use of properties, a wide range of tones from the casual and inconsequential to the ironical and the dramatic. But the true teacher is less self-centered than the actor, more genuinely outgoing, more personally distinct. Although, like the actor with the text of the play, he uses the subject matter of his field as his raw material for his performance, the born teacher feels not only an esthetic but a moral responsibility to the subject matter with which he is working and also to the audience to whom he is presenting this subject matter. In this respect, he more closely resembles the preacher than the actor. Ultimately, he is concerned with bringing light and leading to his charges, with saving them from the sins of ignorance and prejudice, with enriching their lives with knowledge and wisdom. Like the true pastor, he is a "cure of souls." He is concerned with his students not as minds, but as men, not as points on the sliding scale of intellectual achievements, but as human beings with personalities that are curiously complex blends of assets and liabilities, that are bundles of potentialities. Like the pastor, he furnishes—sometimes unwittingly—a kind of norm for behavior and manners, a model, however imperfect, of devotion to the nobler ends of which the human animal dreams and in the attainment of which he is—perhaps fitfully—engaged.

The classification developed here is, obviously, less applicable to members of history and philosophy departments than to members of departments of literature, the fine arts, and music. My experience is too limited to make any classification in the former departments of knowledge of any great weight or significance. The basic distinction between the scholar and the teacher holds good here as well as elsewhere; the incidence of one or another of the variants of the esthetic type is inevitably rare. Historians might well be classified in terms of the breadth or the narrowness of their conception of history. The more "scholarly" the historian, the narrower his interests are likely to be. The broader his interests, the greater likelihood of his being a genuine humanist. Perhaps the narrowest type of historian is the devotee of diplomatic history; a slighter broader type is the specialist in constitutional or economic history; the most broad-minded historians are those who regard all that has happened as their province, who conceive of history as significant in proportion to its inclusiveness, and who have a capacity for synthesizing not only the dynastic, military, and political but the social, esthetic, religious, and philosophical elements in a culture. Philosophers, like others in the humanistic group, have shown a disappointing tendency toward specialization. Their specialization takes the form of an almost exclusive devotion to the interpretation of a particular philosopher (which may be pardoned perhaps when the philosopher is really a major figure) or to the cultivation of a particular branch of philosophy: epistemology, metaphysics, logic, ethics, esthetics, the philosophy of science, the value-theory, and in earlier days, psychology. An interesting variant on the philosophical type, the man who attempts to create a system of his own, is the one most nearly akin to the genuinely creative artist. As teacher, the philosopher demonstrates more clearly than do the members of any other humanistic discipline the close relationship between teaching and preaching. For, whether or not he is overtly the propagandist for a particular school of philosophy, he is much more likely to be conscious of his own private philosophical orientation than the teacher of English or the teacher of history, and, even when he does not actively and vigorously proselytize, he and his personality express his philosophy implicitly and make converts, with or without the conscious expenditure of effort. In America, at least, it is striking that many contemporary teachers of philosophy are the descendants of preachers and have had theological training themselves. The reason for the transition from theology to philosophy is to be found, perhaps, in the decline in moral vigor and spiritual leadership of the Protestant churches in the late nineteenth and twentieth centuries. In consequence, the academic philosopher has tended to take over the functions—advisory, admonitory, confessional—of the clergy of earlier days.

It would be hopelessly idealistic to expect or to hope that a college or university should be able to find for its faculty many men who combine the virtues of the scholar, the artist, and the teacher. The university can afford to seek, and, when found, to encourage good men of each of these types or good men that combine features of at least two of these basic types. Upon the administration of the small college lies the heavy responsibility of preserving a balance of types among the men appointed, or of running the risk of creating an unfortunate imbalance through a tendency to inbreeding. Both university and college administrations would do well to clarify their conceptions of what sorts of faculty members they want and need; these they should seek diligently and reward equally and generously, once they are found.

Another mode of classifying faculty members in the humanistic area that may bring to light some significant characteristics is in terms of their departmental allegiances. Such an objective mode of classification furnishes material for the solution of such questions as the characteristics peculiar to the members of a particular department and the reasons for the apparent superiority of some humanistic departments to other humanistic departments in such qualities as mental vigor, breadth of intellectual interests, and freedom from departmental narrowness and prejudice. Any judgments of faculty members classified according to department on the scale of the qualities just mentioned must of necessity be subjective "value-judgments," and, as such, they are bound to be regarded by some scientific purists as questionable, if not utterly worthless. But since the humanities belong to the area of value and lose their meaning and importance unless their value-aspect is kept constantly in mind, the judgments of a single observer may be worth presenting.

Of the departments considered here as belonging to the humanities—language and literature, fine arts, music, philosophy, and history—I am moved by such experience and observation as have been mine to hold that a descending scale measuring mental vigor, breadth of intellectual interests, and freedom from departmental narrowness would reveal the following order: history, philosophy, fine arts and music, English, and the modern languages.*

Whether or not this ranking of departments has any validity is not at the moment in question; its validity could be established only by comparing the observations and conclusions of a considerable body of competent and experienced observers and analysts. For the moment, it will be sufficient to assume the validity of these conclusions, and to inquire what possible explanations might be found for such conclusions. Such explanations may possibly be found in the nature of the different departmental subject matters and in the demands made by these subject matters upon different types of personalities.

In the case of history, for example, it is not difficult to see that the subject matter is of such a nature as to make

---

* My experience with teachers of the ancient languages has been so meager that I am unwilling to risk placing them on the scale suggested above. I should venture the opinion, however, that the low estate of the ancient languages at the present moment is to be accounted for, not on the ground of the competition with other languages or with subjects in or outside the humanistic field, but on the ground of the temperament and training of men in the classical field. In other words, if the study of the ancient languages is dying out, it is the classicists that have killed the study. The classics remain—imperturbable and timeless—and the persistence of interest in Plato and the extraordinary renaissance of interest in Aristotle in these times indicate perhaps that the philosophers have been more skilled in keeping up interest in their particular authors than the classicists have in the case of Homer and Virgil. The highly specialized and narrowly linguistic training given classicists in the modern graduate school is probably the root of the pitiable plight of classicists and the study of the ancient languages today.

an appeal to at least some individuals of unusual intellectual vigor and with unusually widely ranging interests. History is in and of itself the most broadly inclusive of the humanistic disciplines, since it may legitimately take as its province whatever has happened or, at any rate, whatever has left any evidence of having happened. Since history, moreover, is not merely a subject matter but a method, it may as a method be applied to any sorts of phenomena occurring in time. History, most broadly conceived, may include the historical study of the evolution of domestic utensils, philosophical systems, methods of musical notation, or the making and mixing of colors. It is perhaps possible, as we have seen, for the individual of narrow interests and limited vigor to select some extremely limited aspect of the total historical process, and specialize to his heart's content. But the true historian is tempted to cast a wider and wider net, and, especially since the appearance of the concepts of "the new history" of James Harvey Robinson, or of culture-history generally, he has felt the obligation to attempt the integration and synthesis of the largest possible number of elements in human culture. History, then, challenges its devotees to develop a widely ranging curiosity, a scientific imagination capable of evolving sweeping hypotheses, an historical imagination skilled in the evocation of cultural epochs, and, most of all, the ability to discover the significant patterns made by almost countless specific and perhaps seemingly unrelated phenomena. In the face of these demands, it is not perhaps surprising that history makes its appeal to, and numbers among its devotees, an unusually large proportion of men distinguished by intellectual vigor and breadth of interest.

The appeal of philosophy and its demands are like those of history in breadth but differ from those of history in depth and intensity. For, since the dethroning of theology as the queen of the sciences, philosophy has assumed or should have assumed the throne. Its subject matter is not historical or esthetic or moral or scientific truth but truth generally. Its concern is not with the concrete but with the abstract and the relation between the concrete and the abstract. It is concerned with those unconscious and sometimes forgotten or ignored assumptions that underlie each of the other humanistic disciplines. It is required, therefore, to deal, not with the facts of history, but with the philosophy that underlies the study of history. It is required to deal, not with the interpretation and evaluation of specific works of art but with the nature and function of art generally. Thus, one of its special areas is not the criticism of art but the philosophy of art—esthetics. Unlike religion, which has as one of its functions the proselytizing for particular conceptions of good or evil, philosophy must deal with the general nature of good and of evil. A particular philosophical system may, to be sure, arrive at relatively particular conceptions of good and evil, but the teacher of philosophy, as distinct from the philosopher, must be able to identify himself, temporarily at least, with any logically consistent conceptions of good and evil and must expound them without prejudice or bias. It is certainly arguable and probably demonstrable that two of the basic types of mentality are the historical and the philosophical, and that these types have significant differences, aptitudes, and capacities. At any rate, the philosophically gifted mind is one that moves more easily on the plane of the abstract than the concrete, and that, even though the material with which it works is no more inclusive than that with which the historian works, concentrates on the abstractions implicit in concrete phenomena rather than with generalizations derived from the synthesis of concrete phenomena. It is commonly charged that the contemporary teaching of philosophy has suffered, as all the humanistic disciplines have suffered, from the vice of specialization. There are grounds certainly for this common charge, but there are also grounds for believing that the nature of philosophy itself has prevented the vice of specialization to work such havoc as it has been able to create, for example, in the humanistic disciplines of language and literature.

On the descending scale indicated above—placing the humanistic disciplines in the order in which their adherents manifest intellectual vigor and widely ranging interests—the fine arts and music have been assigned a position midway between history and philosophy at the top and English and the modern languages at the bottom. Assuming that there is some validity in this arrangement, we may ask what the reasons may be for this medial position of the fine arts and music. One reason for their subordination to the positions of history and philosophy may well be the definitely narrower areas of these disciplines. Another reason perhaps is the sometimes conflicting claims and interests of historians and critics and performers in these areas, and the consequently varying demands made upon faculty members devoted to these disciplines. These divergent claims and interests and demands force us to take account of the fact that, not only in fine arts and music but also in literature, the choice among possible approaches to the subject matters of these fields is far more complex than the problem of an approach to either history or philosophy. As a matter of fact, it might be contended that the historian or the philosopher is faced by no choice of a method or a technique of approach. His choice is that of the special area of the whole field in which he is to work. The historical technique or the philosophical technique does not vary significantly, whatever the chosen field may be. On the humanist concerned with the fine arts, music, or literature a more difficult choice is forced. He must decide whether his attack on his special discipline shall be historical, critical, or creative. Whichever choice he makes, he will be working under the esthetic banner, and he will therefore be called upon to exhibit a kind of mentality and sensibility—the esthetic mentality and sensibility—of which the historian and the philosopher may be almost devoid. For it seems certain, in addition to the historical and the philosophical types of mind, there is also the esthetic type of mind—the type that not only approaches the special materials of the fine arts, music, and literature as forms of art, but also tends to view life itself, not so much as a historical process or as a concrete illustration of abstract truths, but as a work of art of which the living man himself is the artist who uses the material of his personality and of his environment as raw material for the creation of a life that shall have the qualities of a work of art: design, proportion, beauty, joy, and significance.*

The choice forced upon devotees of the fine arts and music accounts perhaps for the relative inferiority of these devotees to historians and philosophers in intellectual vigor and breadth of interests. For devotees of these arts have been by no means clear in their own minds as to which of the possible attacks upon their special subject matters—the historical, the critical, or the creative—is the more promising and meaningful. If the devotees of fine arts and music rank above the devotees of various literatures in vigor and breadth, one reason may be that departments of fine arts and music would feel themselves exceedingly poverty-stricken if they could not boast of including some creative or interpretive artists. It would certainly be agreed that it is far more usual to find a painter in a department of fine

* This view of life as a work of art or as a potential work of art is set forth eloquently in Havelock Ellis' *The dance of life* (Houghton Mifflin, 1923). One of its most suggestive chapters is that on "The art of thought" in which Ellis presents the philosopher as an artist, that is to say, as a man who finds his deepest satisfaction in creating art-like systems out of ideas rather than out of sounds or colors or sensory impressions.

arts than to find a professional writer in a department of English. The habit of such inclusions in departments of fine arts and the encouragement of such a habit by the Carnegie Corporation account to a very considerable degree for the kind of vitality one feels in such departments. For the artist, as we have already seen, brings a special kind of vigor and perception and insight, not only to his colleagues but also to the students fortunate enough to work with him. Whatever his deficiencies as a teacher may be, the artist, as a man dedicated to the creation of works of art, is a singularly potent cultural symbol.

The presence of creative artists in departments of fine arts and music is not, however, the sole element that accounts for the superiority in vigor and breadth of interests of these departments over departments of literature. Another element is the superior resistance these subject matters have offered to the historical attack. A painting, a piece of sculpture, or a sonata is, on the one hand, a seemingly more accessible object for analysis, interpretation, and criticism, and, on the other hand, less immediately suitable material for treatment as an historical document. The fine arts and music invite the analytical-critical attack as a work of literature apparently does not. It seems more appropriate to analyze the structure of a sonata and to distinguish its qualities in relation to other sonatas than to treat it as a document in the history of the sonata type or in the evolution of the creative life of the composer. Despite the fact that the historical method has already done almost irreparable damage to the study of the fine arts and music, they have been protected from the worst devastations of the historical scavenger by the presence of artists in these departments and the more conspicuously "esthetic" nature of the subject matters of these departments.

That faculty members in the departments of English literature and the other modern literatures should rate lowest on a scale of intellectual vigor and breadth of extra-departmental interests is not difficult to explain, since it is these departments that have taken over most enthusiastically the historical-scientific method and have been most diligent in training college and university teachers in this method exclusively. Moreover, the accessibility of the materials in these departments and the almost universal habit of reading (though reading very badly) have lured into English departments particularly a large number of intellectually flabby or one-track-minded individuals who go into the teaching of English because they are unwilling to meet the challenges of more inaccessible materials or more difficult methods. It is a matter of common observation that a large number of undergraduates major in English because they have no well-defined interests or because they do not feel intellectually equal to the demands of history or philosophy, and much less of the social or the natural sciences. There is every reason to believe that a great many men and women embark upon the teaching of English for no more respectable motives. English departments also suffer particularly from the abundance of the material with which they feel it necessary to deal. It would be difficult to find a reputable graduate school that did not make some pretense of requiring all its candidates for the doctor's degree to show some acquaintance with the whole field of English literature, and to possess at least a reading knowledge of one, two, or three other languages in addition. If graduate schools and undergraduate colleges, for that matter, were to train students in the various techniques for attacking literature—historical, linguistic, analytical, and critical—instead of forcing them to acquaint themselves with an enormous body of subject matter and to become experts in a narrow area of that matter, the products of colleges and universities would have a better opportunity than they now have for the cultivation of extra-departmental interests. The extent of the demands made upon graduate students in the field of English is such that most heads of graduate departments are forced to develop a set of defense mechanisms against the claims of other humanistic departments for some place in the training of students of English language and literature.

To assign the teachers of modern languages to the lowest place on the scale measuring intellectual vigor and breadth of intellectual interests is a hazardous proceeding. One's only protection against charges of prejudice and bias is the indication not of the personal grounds for such a judgment but of the possible reasons that make such a judgment comprehensible. Certainly one of the comprehensible reasons for such a judgment is the fact that faculty members in these departments are required by the nature of our educational system to devote so much of their time to introducing students to the earlier stages of the language. The modern language teacher is in a position that parallels the teacher of English to adult aliens or the teacher in the elementary school introducing natives to the fearful wonders of English spelling, grammar, and vocabulary. Of neither the teacher of language to alien adults or the teacher of English to infants is demanded a complex culture or widely ranging intellectual interests. The devotion of many years or a considerable part of one's program for many years to elementary language work is as intellectually deadening an experience as a similar regimen of teaching elementary English composition. Any person who flourishes on such a regimen is rather likely to be unimaginative and uninspired; any person who endures such a regimen is likely to be deadened by it or possibly embittered. Another reason for the poor showing of modern language teachers is their own preoccupation with language as language rather than with language as a means of introducing the student to a major mode of expression of a country's life and thought. The person who is interested in the development of language as a skill is likely to be so absorbed in developing that skill that he has little time or energy for a functional approach to the language. Even when he does have an interest in the literature for which the skill in language is an indispensable approach, his interest in the culture of which the language is a part is likely to be no wider than the interest of his colleagues in the department of English. The language of a country plus its literature does not constitute the total culture of a country, but many teachers of modern languages seem to act on the opposite assumption. The use of language skill to introduce the student to the whole range of the scientific, philosophical, social, and esthetic aspects of a culture is all too rare a phenomenon in modern language teaching.

Whatever one's judgments may be as to the possession by faculty members in the humanistic departments of intellectual vigor and extended extra-departmental interests, it would be difficult to find any but the most complacent members of the profession who would hold that the personnel in the humanities field could not easily be improved. We may, therefore, conclude this discussion of academic personnel by suggesting a number of ways in which the quality of teachers in the field of the humanities might be enhanced.

The first—and perhaps the most important—of these suggestions is that more care ought to be taken by deans of graduate schools and the heads of humanities departments in the selection of academic personnel for training in these disciplines. The Carnegie Foundation's "Pennsylvania study" of college graduates intending to become teachers has revealed shockingly the inferior quality of a large proportion of these academic aspirants.* This condition would seem to go far toward establishing the truth or the half-truth of Bernard Shaw's observation that "He who can, does; he who can't, teaches." The admission of inferior human material to graduate schools and teachers' colleges is the fact primarily responsible for the relatively low quality of much academic personnel. If one looks for the reasons for such negligence at the very point where selectivity could operate with least human wastage, one is likely to find one cause, at any rate, in the high degree of competitiveness that has developed among teachers' colleges on the one hand, and graduate schools on the other. The multiplication of graduate schools and teachers' colleges out of all proportion to the needs of at least the more prosperous sections of our country is the factor that encourages this unscrupulous competition. The low quality of the human material undergoing training in many teachers' colleges is part and parcel of the unhealthy and sinister conditions that create and maintain many of these public institutions. The teachers' college, like the public school, is frequently the happy hunting ground of the more unscrupulous type of local politician, who plays on the local pride and the economic self-interest of the area he represents to keep such an institution going. Another influence that keeps the teachers' college flourishing is that of the department of education in some state universities. Such an influence may be exerted for good or for ill; frequently its philosophy is one that is alien to the philosophy of humanism, if not outspokenly hostile to it. The vested interests of educationalists and the influence of these interests are in very large part responsible for the quality of at least the lower ranges of the teaching profession today.

The privately endowed graduate school would seem to

* For the statistics supporting this conclusion, see Chapter III, endnote 3.

be relatively immune from those pressures that tend to develop the spirit of unscrupulous competition. But the overabundance of graduate schools has brought about a situation that has had unfortunate effects on the quality of the academic profession. For a graduate school justifies its existence, primarily, by the number of M.A.'s and Ph.D.'s it produces, and, secondarily, by the amount, if not the quality, of the publications turned out by its faculty members and its graduates.[4] Since this is the case, it is not to be wondered at that graduate schools compete for students as avidly as do undergraduate colleges, and, once they have secured such students, tend to encourage them—unless they are quite hopeless—to continue their work until it is crowned by the doctor's degree. Heads of graduate departments are frequently inhumanly callous in their concern as to whether the graduates they produce can be "placed," or will perform effectively when they have been placed.[5] Whatever the origin of the privately endowed graduate school, it ought to feel itself free from some of the grosser pressures, ought to feel itself free to limit its numbers and to give the very best men and women it can get the best training that it can devise. Anyone who is familiar with the actual operation of even our most distinguished graduate schools will acknowledge how far short they fall of this ideal.

The improvement of humanities personnel is possible not only through a more discriminating selectivity by the deans and heads of departments in graduate schools but also in terms of the ends and objectives, not only of the graduate school but of the liberal arts college. It is perhaps too much to hope that in the near future graduate schools will modify their objectives to include the training not only of scholars but of teachers. All the more heavy, then, is the responsibility of the presidents and heads of departments in a liberal arts college of choosing candidates in the light of the needs of a particular department and of the college generally. A properly balanced department or a college faculty, for that matter, should include proportionate elements of scholars, artists, and teachers. Unfortunately, the prestige of degrees and of publications is still so great that the faculties of most small liberal arts colleges show a preponderance of scholars at the expense of the artists and the teachers. This preponderance is due, moreover, to the lack of clarity in the minds of college presidents and faculties as to the distinction between the functions of a college and a university. Most small colleges tend to ape the universities in their insistence that their faculty must be not only good teachers but also productive scholars. The ideal condition, to be sure, would perhaps be a faculty made up of men who were equally scholars, teachers, and artists. But since such men are extraordinarily few, the part of wisdom would seem to be the attempt to secure and to maintain a balanced faculty, one which boasts of its excellent scholars but which is also known for the favor it shows to men who are artists or primarily teachers. If a marked change in the objectives and methods of the graduate school is not to be hoped for, the presidents and deans of small liberal arts colleges have a very special responsibility in providing their students with men skilled in the various techniques that have been developed for the presentation of the humanities.

Protests against the conventional training for the doctorate have become so numerous and so insistent that possibly the chance that the graduate schools may respond to these pressures is greater than one thinks. The change, if it comes, is not likely to be spectacular because the vested interests of scholars in their highly specialized subjects constitute an almost insurmountable obstacle to even a modest reform. There are, however, some indications of a stirring of the stagnant waters. The fact that some of our older and more influential institutions are making it possible to combine training in history and literature or literature and fine arts is an indication that the now almost universal disapprobation of excessive departmentalization has made itself felt. The desiccation and drouth that have manifested themselves in certain fields such as linguistics, the classics, and medieval studies and the vitality that is showing itself in such fields of study as modern European history, modern philosophy, post-impressionistic painting, nineteenth-century English literature, and American history and literature are, likewise, indications of a promising kind of growth and development. The dissatisfaction with the narrow and rigid fields of specialization in the study of literature—a specialization perfectly illustrated by the conventional categories that are part and parcel of the traditional organization of the Modern Language Association of America—shows itself in the multiplication of more or less generously tolerated experimental categories that indicate a reaching out for wider syntheses and the exploitation of significant relationships.*

There is a final means by which personnel in the field of the humanities and in other fields as well might be improved. Since the graduate schools have been openly contemptuous of "education" and "teacher-training," they have almost utterly neglected what one might suppose would be one of their major obligations—the training of teachers for careers in undergraduate colleges.[6] They have been complacently satisfied with the training of scholars; they have unimaginatively assumed that a good scholar is bound to make a good teacher, although a little self-scrutiny and personal reminiscence would convince them that the good scholar who is a good teacher is a very rare bird

* I have in mind the comparatively recent appearance of such groups as Literature and Society, Esthetics and Literary Form, or even Anglo-French Literary Relations.

indeed; they have regarded any curiosity about teaching techniques or any scrutiny of the ends or methods appropriate to undergraduate education as beneath their contempt. In consequence, the fledgling Ph.D. altogether too frequently confronts his first classes with no guidance or experience in the art and craft of the teaching profession. The great teacher, to be sure, is "born," not made, but the potentially good teacher might profit much from some form of deliberate and critical apprenticeship in his great craft. Some such training might have the result, not merely of improving the quality of teaching in the more elementary classes in the college curriculum, but also of developing the habit of interest and curiosity with regard to educational objectives and methods generally. Since most of the college teachers in this century have been trained as scholars, since they have been encouraged to be narrowly departmental in their thinking and interests, it is no wonder that one of the most prevalent of occupational diseases is the absence of any concern with either the purposes of the liberal arts colleges as a whole or with the means by which such purposes, when agreed upon, may be most effectively attained. If the liberal arts college itself has lost a sense of its major functions and objectives, if department members no longer see the relationship between their departmental labors and the total performance of the college, certainly one of the reasons for this decline in *esprit de corps* and for the increasingly atomistic philosophy that underlies higher education is the failure of the men trained in graduate schools to have any vision of the systematic relationships of the humanistic disciplines to each other and to the nonhumanistic disciplines.

CHAPTER V

THE FUTURE OF THE HUMANITIES

THERE are grounds for considerable hope that the humanities are in many places and in many ways undergoing a process of rejuvenation and revitalization. But such experiments and innovations, while encouraging and promising, will fail of complete effectiveness unless certain larger tasks are undertaken by enthusiastic humanists. Such larger tasks are the more pressing since the crisis in liberal education brought about by the war is a threat not merely to the programs and procedures already under way but to the very existence of liberal education. It is not an accurate measure of the esteem in which liberal education is held in the United States that not only the military authorities but the heads of great universities should be willing to call a halt to liberal education during the war emergency; that President Day of Cornell can say, without any feeling of embarrassment, that "liberal education is out for the duration"; and that Dean Gauss of Princeton can maintain that a knowledge of Plato does not make a man a better soldier. What we have witnessed without really being aware of it is *la trahison des clercs*, as Benda picturesquely called it, the desertion of American education by the men who should have been its defenders to the last ditch.

Where the leaders of liberal education in America had any genuine understanding of its significance or appreciation of its ends, it was impossible for them to throw it overboard at the drop of a brass hat. Liberal education is *not* a commodity like coffee that can be rationed for the duration. It is rather something, like breathing, without which life cannot go on. Liberal education is not something that can be laid on the shelf for the five or ten years of a world war; liberal education, if it is anything, is a process that must continue without interruption. It is a process that must be nurtured and encouraged under the most dispiriting circumstances. Any complete cessation in liberal education would mean a kind of death for our civilization.

Fortunately, the round utterances of a few persons in high places are bound to exhibit that elementary two-valued orientation against which the semanticists have warned us. For the sake of publicity and for the purposes of making their positions clear to the public or military mind, they must state their case in black and white terms that seriously misrepresent the facts. Liberal education is not out for the duration so long as it is proceeding anywhere under even the most difficult circumstances. Those liberal arts colleges which tighten their belts and keep going without subsidization by either the federal government or the armed services may well prove centers in which the lights of civilization are kept burning, flames in scattered shrines in the midst of a world given over to the barbarism of technological warfare. But, if such shrines are to be kept alight, if such shrines are to draw worshipers to them in increasing numbers after the war, their high priests and acolytes must see to it that their lamps are clean and their flames pure.

The major task of those who believe in liberal education is a clarification of the objectives of that education. It is notorious that the liberal arts college is unsure of its objectives, has lost sight of its purposes. It is notorious that in most such institutions it would be difficult for the administration and the members of the faculty to agree on what their major functions are. There are innumerable reasons why the liberal arts college should have lost sight of its goal. Some of these reasons have been indicated and explained in earlier chapters: the multiplication of courses in the liberal arts curriculum and their struggle to become the fittest to survive, the primacy of science and the scientific method in the twentieth-century climate of opinion, the pressure of professionalism and vocationalism, and the attempts of professional educationalists to subdue liberal education to their own purposes. The goals of liberal education have been peculiarly obscured in the public and private universities, where the college of liberal arts—under whatever name—is submitted to pressures from all sides, and where it maintains its own identity, integrity, and philosophy only with the greatest difficulty. Although the small liberal arts college may seem, in some respects, to be an ivory tower or may seem—ostrich-like—to keep what head it has deep in the sands of time, it is relatively free from pressures and therefore the more responsible for the definition and clarification of its purposes.

An additional reason, however, for the failure of even the small liberal arts college to define and clarify its purposes is the uncertainty as to where the responsibility for defining such a policy lies. Does it lie with the trustees, the president, or the faculty? On the answer to this question there seems to be no common agreement. What is at any rate clear is that the presidents of American colleges have failed signally in furnishing light and leading as to the purposes and functions of the institutions over which they preside. It would be a fruitful subject for speculation and investigation to inquire why the "leadership" furnished by college presidents has been so uninspired and conventional. From how few college presidents does one expect to get more than the most obvious banalities about the significance of the processes over which they preside!

Certainly one of the reasons for the "dim-bulb" quality

of the leadership furnished by most American college presidents is the fact that higher education in America has not only become one of our major business enterprises but has taken on many of the characteristics of "big business." In other words, the typical college president is not easily distinguishable from the chairman of the board of a corporation. From such a figure, we hardly expect intellectual insight and illumination. Instead, we expect him to report that the college accounts have been carefully checked by experts, and that the college's books do or do not balance. A good president, therefore, is not a great thinker about the processes of education but a skillful business man who keeps the institution's plant in good condition, its workmen in a state of placid unrebelliousness, and his business out of the red. The typical American college president has, in other words, become the business agent of the board of trustees, and it is certainly not the function of the business agent to raise questions as to the value of the product of the business. Probably the college's taking on the character of a business enterprise goes a considerable distance in explaining why the intellectual caliber of most college presidents is distressingly low. Another reason for the timorous and tepid nature of most presidential utterances is the fact that, in addition to keeping the college books balanced, the president is the person primarily responsible for the public relations of the college. He is therefore compelled to censor his utterances so that no powerful group in the community in which the college is known shall be seriously offended.

If in the nature of the case, college presidents have signally failed in defining and clarifying the objectives of liberal education, one may very well ask why college faculties have not assumed the responsibility. Perhaps the most important reason for this failure has been that process of departmentalization as a result of which the practitioners of each subject have become guardians of a special vested interest, and in the protection of it, have lost sight of the place of this interest in the larger scheme of liberal arts education and thus of the general purposes of liberal arts education itself. For the reasons just indicated, the responsibility for keeping clear the purposes and goals of liberal arts education has not been satisfactorily discharged. It would be impertinent for me to attempt such a definition and clarification, but some of the tasks involved may perhaps be suggested.

Primarily, the purposes of liberal arts education must be distinguished from the purposes of professional and vocational education. Obviously, in contrast to professional and vocational education, its purposes are nonutilitarian. It does not, and should not, teach men and women how to earn a living. But, if it does not teach men and women how to make a better living than they would make without such education, what does it do? What can it offer to a predominantly utilitarian and pragmatic social order? It does, and it should, teach men and women how to make, not better livings, but better lives. It achieves, or attempts to achieve, this objective by developing, not the student's mechanical or technical or even organizational and managerial capacities, but his intellectual, esthetic, and spiritual powers. The liberal arts college—above all the other institutional organizations in our society—is that which should serve as a refuge and stronghold, a nursery, of those values that are definitely nonutilitarian.

The values that should be developed by liberal arts education might be clarified if educators attempted to distinguish between those common to the disciplines of the natural sciences, the social sciences, and the humanities, and those peculiar to each of these disciplines.[1]

130

The general values common to all liberal disciplines, or disciplines that are capable of being pursued in the liberal spirit, are the reduction of ignorance, the increase of information, the minimizing of prejudice and the enhancement of tolerance, the development of respect for facts and training in distinguishing between what is and what is not a fact, a respect for logic and a devotion to its application in areas to which it is pertinent and a rejection of it in areas to which it is not pertinent, an awareness of the past and its influence upon the present, a comprehension of the dominant character of the contemporary society, and a conception of the complexity of the world in which we live and of the human beings and institutions in that world.

But the objectives and purposes of liberal education could be even more clearly seen if educators were to define, not only the general goals of such education, but also the specific contributions to such education that are most likely to be made by the major intellectual disciplines. The attempt to bring some sort of order out of the intellectual chaos resulting from the proliferation of subject matters and departments has led to a fairly common agreement as to what those major disciplines are. It has now become conventional to distinguish the fields of the natural sciences, the social sciences, and the humanities.[2] The now widespread practice of grouping departments into divisions (or schools) may or may not have any meaning. Sometimes, it is no more than a casual gesture made in the direction of bringing some sort of order into the agglomeration of departmental interests. More frequently, it is of use merely to indicate the various fields over which the student must maintain a superficial "distribution." In most cases, it is extremely doubtful whether the divisional organization has enhanced the sense of intellectual interests common to members of the faculty within a particular division. But the divisional organization, the broad distinctions made among fields of knowledge, offer an admirable opportunity to consider what purposes and objectives are peculiar to a particular division or field and more or less completely distinct from the purposes and objectives of other fields.[3] This is not the occasion nor am I competent to work out in detail or with precision the purposes and objectives peculiar to the major fields of knowledge, but at least some broad, if tentative, distinctions can be made.

The peculiar subject matter of the physical sciences is the universe exclusive of man.[4] The objective of the pure physical scientist might be stated, quite simply, as the pushing forward of the boundaries of information concerning the nature of the physical universe. He will be forced to deal with such problems as the nature of matter and energy, and chemical elements, and the history of the physical universe, and to evolve hypotheses concerning the principles of its operation, and to establish these principles as "laws" by the application of the scientific method to the available data. The objective in teaching the physical sciences in the liberal arts college is the orientation of the student in the physical universe, the deepening of his understanding of the nonorganic, nonhuman world in which his existence is to be lived. In this nonhuman world, human values are irrelevant and intrusive, but the acquaintance with this nonhuman world and its unmitigated impersonality is one of the most salutary of the student's intellectual experiences, the experience most calculated perhaps to give him a sense of proportion and an awareness of the insignificance of himself and his kind.[5] In the nature of the case, the physical sciences are the least humane and, therefore, the most resistant to complete assimilation into a program of humane studies, and it is not to be wondered at that there is a more or less conscious hostility between humanists and physical scientists.*

The subject matter of the biological sciences is organic life, human and subhuman. Like the physical scientist, the biological scientist is concerned with evolving hypotheses pertaining to the principles of operation of organic life, and with establishing these principles as "laws" by the application of the scientific method to the available data. But as a biological scientist, he is particularly concerned with such problems as evolution, heredity, the structure and substance of animal bodies, reproduction, health and disease, the nature and behavior of the mind, the nervous bases of behavior, and the character and conditions of mental activity. Strictly speaking, in so far as he is concerned with man, he conceives of him, not as a human being but as an animal, and his tendency is to stress the similarities between man and other animals rather than their differences. The teacher of the biological sciences aims to contribute to the student's "understanding of the role of the human organism in the world of life," to give him an "account of the nature and history of living organisms," and to make him "aware of his own nature, considered from a broad biological point of view." [6]

The proper subject matter of the social sciences is man as a social being. The social scientist finds his material for observation and generalization in the behavior of human beings in groups; that is, in political, economic, and broadly social relationships. Since the group activities of human beings find their causes in the psychological needs and desires

* Aside from the conflict between the nonhuman interests of the physical scientists and the human interests of the humanists, there is an added reason for their inclination to estrangement. The pure scientist is under constant pressure to become an applied scientist, and thus he is subjected to all the influences that operate in our pre-eminently technological society. Like the social scientist, he is constantly tempted to co-operate with industrial enterprise, and to adapt himself to its *mores*.

of human beings, the social scientist finds himself faced with a material that is compact with values, and that, therefore, is much more resistant to scientific manipulation than the material with which the physical scientist or even the biological scientist deals. To give his work the character of science, the modern social scientist has developed the statistical method, which is intended to eliminate or at least to minimize the subjective element conspicuous in the predominantly analytical activities of the earlier social scientists.[7]

In the classroom, the social scientist attempts "(1) to develop in the student an appreciation of our society as a 'going concern'; (2) to make clear some of the significant characteristics of modern social organization in this country; (3) to point out the nature of social change and social problems; and (4) to describe some of the current efforts to solve these problems."[8]

The functions and purposes peculiar to the humanities are less easy to define than those of the sciences, whether physical, biological, or social, and yet no task facing the humanist is perhaps quite so pressing and so crucial as this definition and clarification of function.[9] One of the reasons for this difficulty is that the subject matters that compose the humanities are less obviously coherent than those that comprise any one of the groups of sciences. The factors common to literature, fine arts, music, history, philosophy, and religion are not so easy to designate as those common, for example, to zoology, biology, and botany. There is, moreover, a historical reason for the lack of clarity in the objectives of the humanities. Historically, the sciences— whether physical or social—are descendants of one or another of the major humanistic disciplines. Thus, philosophy is the ultimate source, not only of the modern science of psychology but of "natural philosophy," which in turn is the parent of both the physical and the biological sciences.

134

In the same way, the social sciences may be said to be the offspring of history and ethics, since they represent, in the historical phase, highly specialized forms of history and, in their ethical phase, specialized forms of behavior, more or less "good." The conception of a "healthy" society is obviously one that is grounded on an ideal, whether sound or not, basically ethical. The result of this growing genealogical complexity is that the parent-stock tends to be regarded as a kind of obsolete residue, an intellectual remnant less significant than its young and sturdy and independent descendants.

Despite the complexity and obscurity of the problem, it is possible, however, to indicate the special characteristics of the humanities and to designate their most important functions. The element common to the humanities is their common concern with values. "With human consciousness," the biologist Julian Huxley has said, "values and ideals appeared on earth for the first time." * Values, however, are not the concern of the humanities alone. There are values common to the sciences and the humanities, as there are values peculiar to both these groups of disciplines. But it is possible and necessary to contend that the disciplines represent a scale of values, and that the humanities are unequivocally at the top of that scale.

The physical sciences—at least in their pure state—are lowest in intrinsic human values. I cannot see that there is any human significance in whatever facts may be arrived at concerning the nature of the atom or the number of stars in the universe. There are unquestionably extrinsic intellectual values in the curiosity that lies behind quests for such factual knowledge and in the ingenuity and patience involved in developing techniques for arriving at scientific truths, but the truths themselves are devoid of *human* sig-

* Quoted in *Time*, December 14, 1942, p. 65, from his article in *Fortune*, December, 1942.

nificance. With the application of the physical sciences, the case is altered, but the most energetic application of the physical sciences can hardly do more than effect changes—spectacular and momentous, to be sure—in man's physical environment. Such changes may or may not modify man's system of human values. There is obviously no correlation—unless it is an inverse correlation—between changes in man's physical environment and in his moral and esthetic character. The most violent alterations of man's environment do not seem to have increased the number of great or of good men.[10] On the scale of human values, the biological sciences rank higher than the physical sciences. But, since their concern is with man as an animal, their rank on the scale of human values must remain below the social sciences and the humanities. In the biologist's conception of physical health and the psychologist's conception of mental health, there are obviously values pertinent to human existence. The biologist's conception of physical health is obviously pertinent not only to the individual but to the community, and it would be granted without question that physical health is one of the basic "goods" with which human beings are concerned. But it is a more elementary and naive form of "good" than that implicit in the social sciences and the humanities. Similarly, the psychologist's conception of mental health is pertinent to both the individual and the community, but his conception—particularly if he is a physiological psychologist—is likely to be even more naive and unphilosophical than that of the biologist.

The social sciences come closest to the humanities on the scale of human values, but, since their concern is primarily with man as a social being and not as an individual, they must take second place at least in a society which has as its goal the development of the potentialities of as many gifted individuals as possible. In the nature of their subject

136

matter, moreover, the social scientists are concerned with the behavior of groups or with norms of behavior rather than with the behavior of highly gifted or extraordinary individuals. The values brought to human existence by the poet or the saint will always remain inaccessible to statistical treatment. Furthermore, since the conception of a healthy society or a good society is an ethical conception, the social scientist must depend ultimately for his notion of goodness on his own usually imperfect analysis or will derive his notion of goodness from a philosopher, a professional expert in such an analysis.*

On the scale of human values, the humanities rank highest because these disciplines are primarily concerned, not merely with physical or social values, but with individual and humane values.[11] The objective of the humanities might very well be stated in Julian Huxley's terms, "the quest for truth and knowledge, virtue, beauty and esthetic expression, and its satisfaction through the channels of . . . philosophy, mysticism and morality, literature and the arts." †

The objectives of the humanities may perhaps be distinguished more clearly if we bear in mind the fact that, while they embrace different kinds of disciplines, all the disciplines deal primarily with humane values.[12] The disciplines that belong to the humanities fall into three clearly defined groups: the esthetic, the moral and intellectual, and the historical. Each of these groups makes its special approach to the problem of value.[13]

History is at once a subject matter and a method. To the

* The naïveté of both the biologist and the psychologist may be suggested by the fact that a very "good" man may produce a very "bad" book and a very "unhealthy" man may be a very "good" philosopher. To most psychologists, most of the saints and prophets would probably appear as reprehensible neurotics, or worse.

† Quoted in *Time*, December 14, 1942, p. 65, from his article in *Fortune*, December, 1942.

humanities, history as subject matter is more significant than history as a method. As a subject, history "concerns itself with everything that man has ever done, individually or collectively, but especially with those things which contribute to an understanding of man and his institutions and ideals." The values of history, as distinct from the historical method, are many, but in particular history serves the humanist by giving perspective to the limited experience of modern man, by developing tolerance for alien modes of personality, behavior, and culture, by revealing the forces that have shaped the personalities of human beings and created the social order which more or less perfectly satisfies their needs and hopes, and meets the challenge of their ideals.*

Literature, the fine arts, and music constitute a group of humanistic disciplines with strikingly similar objectives and functions.[14] "The arts," I. A. Richards has said, "are our storehouse of recorded values. They spring from and perpetuate hours in the lives of exceptional people, when their control and command of experience is at its highest, hours when the varying possibilities of existence are most clearly seen and the different activities which may arise are most exquisitely reconciled, hours when habitual narrowness of interests and confused bewilderment are replaced by an intricately wrought composure. Both in the genesis of a work of art, in the creative moment, and in its aspect as a vehicle

---

* Among the humanistic disciplines, history is probably the one that is least concerned with values, because of its dual nature as a science and an art. As a science, it is primarily concerned with what happened; as an art, it is concerned with the significance or value or meaning of what happened. Because it devotes itself to solving both these problems, the service of history to the humanities is, or may be, only halfhearted. Since the historical method—that is, the scientific method applied to historical material—has tended to become the primary means of attack of the other humanistic disciplines, it has, therefore, rendered a disservice in obscuring what should be the primary method of attack, namely, an analysis and discrimination of values.

138

of communication, reasons can be found for giving the arts a very important place in the theory of Value. They record the most important judgments we possess as to the values of experience . . . The arts, if rightly approached, supply the best data available for deciding what experiences are more valuable than others." * The arts, in other words, express in their varying media whatever experience, real or imagined, whatever feeling, emotion, or idea, creative personalities have judged most worthy of permanent expression.[15]

The arts, like the other humanistic disciplines, can be approached historically, but a major or exclusive emphasis on the historical approach to the arts is a denial, if not a betrayal, of their particular function. For, while every artist lives in time and, living in time, is shaped by the circumstances and the esthetic and intellectual climate of his era, his work, if it is sufficiently vital to continue an active existence, has value, not merely as a skillful precipitation of his experience in his chosen medium, but rather as an enduring and always accessible expression of experiences that are of value to persons of any epoch. It is the fact that works of art, produced in one period, survive and continue to have a more than historical value through many succeeding periods, that makes the most significant approach to their study, not historical, but analytical and critical. Thus, it is legitimate and profitable to study Racine's *Phèdre* as a supreme expression of seventeenth-century culture; it is more significant and pertinent to analyze such a masterpiece for the values—technical and imaginative and moral— that it still yields the skillful and trained reader.†

* I. A. Richards, *The principles of literary criticism* (Harcourt, Brace, 1924), pp. 32-33.
† Certainly one of the unfortunate effects of the application of the historical method to the arts is that of giving a kind of artificial and galvanized life to the minor works of earlier periods, works which may have a considerable historical value and may illuminate the study

As Richards has indicated, the arts "supply the best data available for deciding what experiences are more valuable than others," but only if they are "properly approached." He adds, "Happily there is no lack of glaring examples to remind us of the difficulty of approaching them rightly." *
This is not the place to raise the question of the problems involved in arriving at the principles of right criticism nor even for setting forth any particular critical method. But it seems obvious, from the indications already made as to the nature of the material of works of art and of their media, that no narrow or limited or exclusive critical theory will serve to bring to light the Protean values the arts embrace. No critical method can be deemed satisfactory unless it takes into account all the aspects of the work of art, not merely its technique but also the emotional, intellectual, and moral aspects of its subject matter. Only such all-inclusive criticism can be counted on to bring to light the myriad facets of the values embodied in works of art.

Religion and philosophy obviously belong within the fold of the humanistic studies, since both these manifestations of the human spirit are eminently concerned with humane values.

In the course of his struggle for survival the human has distinguished himself from the other animals in his effort to explain the universe in which he lives and his relationship to it. His effort has brought into existence religion, science, and philosophy. The first and most primitive of these, religion, is both intellectual and emotional, for it not only seeks to explain the nature of the universe, but also gives expression to

of history, but which no longer have any very conspicuous values for modern man. From this point of view, the insistence of President Hutchins and the administration of St. John's College that students ought to study only major works of the mind and the imagination is a healthy corrective to the kind of selectivity or unselectivity that results from considerations largely historical.

* Richards, *op. cit.*, p. 33.

the aspiration of men to live in harmony with the forces that govern the universe. Thus the animism of the primitive savage is at one with the highly sophisticated religion of Augustine or Thomas Aquinas in its effort at once to explain the nature of the world intellectually and to bring men to a sense of emotional peace. This thread of wonder and aspiration is without doubt one of the most persistent and one of the most powerful forces in the development of civilization. . . .

Older than science, but closely related to both science and religion, philosophy—as the effort by purely intellectual processes to explain the nature of all existence, humanity included—has had its own important role in the history of civilized man. . . . Philosophy, "mother of all the sciences," draws upon both religion and science—indeed, upon the entire body of human knowledge—for its materials. It has neither the emotion of religion nor the empiricism of science; yet, as the apex of the intellectual pyramid, it is the crowning intellectual achievement of mankind.*

The distinctive subject matter of philosophy C. J. Ducasse has defined as "the demands of the human will-to-values. The typical varieties of these demands, their essential natures, their mutual relations, the sorts of objective conditions which the satisfaction of them postulates, are the questions which philosophy, and philosophy alone, sets itself to investigate with scientific care. The results of such investigations it attempts to formulate in classifications, definitions, postulates, and theorems, which together constitute the philosophy of the particular subject to which they relate. And the knowledge which they embody is knowledge not of Nature but of what is *a priori* to Nature, for it is knowledge of what man intends, demands, values, or means, as distinguished from what he simply confronts." †

* Quoted from the Preface to the syllabus of the Stanford University course in the History of Western Civilization.

† C. J. Ducasse, *The relation of philosophy to education* (Unpublished manuscript), p. 51.

Certainly in the hierarchy of humanistic subjects philosophy should occupy the central and crucial place, since philosophy alone can furnish that systematic investigation of values that will insure the proper and healthy emphasis on all the subjects in the liberal arts curriculum.[16]

Professor Ducasse has stated the case for such primacy persuasively. "The position of philosophy is unique in kind because philosophy studies a type of subject-matter different from that of either the natural or social sciences, or the arts and literature. But it may also be asserted that, in an education which attempts to be liberal, the study of philosophy is unique in importance as well as in kind. This is so because the freedom of thought, the versatility of outlook, and the catholicity of appreciation, which philosophy alone deliberately and systematically cultivates as an end, constitute the very essence of what is called a liberal attitude. If these contentions are correct, there are then good objective grounds . . . for giving philosophy a unique place in the liberal arts curriculum. This will mean, not placing it with other subjects in a group from which election of one is required of the student, but rather frankly recognizing the fact that philosophy constitutes a distinct group, of which it is the only member, and indeed one which, because of its nature, forms the very foundation of a liberal attitude." [17]

If our analysis of the values peculiar to the various groups of disciplines is sound, it should be clear that, among these groups, humanistic studies ought to be given prime place in any well-built liberal curriculum. Unless they are allotted a central and fundamental position among liberal arts studies, and unless they maintain this position vigorously and influentially, liberal arts education will be shadow rather than substance. Furthermore, unless all the members of a college faculty honestly hold that such an allotted position is the *sine qua non* of liberal education, that education will be a counterfeit and not a reality.

But the task of the humanist is not limited to defining and establishing the values of humanistic studies and their primacy among the studies in the liberal curriculum. His more difficult and unending task is to see to it that men are trained who will not debilitate the humanistic tradition, but will constantly vitalize it. In this connection, his duty is to see to it that men of the right sort are encouraged to undertake training for careers as humanists and that the right sort of training is provided for them.

In the attainment of these ends, two procedures suggest themselves. The first is negative. The humanist must do all in his power to destroy the incubus of the old-line graduate school—the major source of illiberalism in liberal studies. The chief source of the strength of the graduate schools' grip upon liberal education is the weight given to their degrees by college and university administrators and by certifying bodies which measure the effectiveness of an institution by the number of Ph.D.'s on the faculty. Neither college administrators nor certifying bodies, usually made up of professors of education, are likely to possess much capacity for discriminating between scholars, pedants, and humanists. It is therefore the duty of faculty members who hold humanism in high esteem to use their influence and intelligence to counteract the tendency to measure a man's worth by the number of degrees he possesses. At the moment, humanistic studies in American graduate schools are in such low repute—even among scholars—that it is extremely difficult to advise a bright promising student which academic guillotine to choose. A persistent and widespread refusal to require this treadmill training of young men interested in teaching would gradually make the light dawn on even the purblind eyes of graduate deans and faculties. The humanist, further, can bring his influence to bear directly upon such deans and faculties by appealing to them to reconsider their objectives and methods and to experiment with new methods designed to encompass new objectives.* Such pressure might, in the long run, gradually bring about major alterations in the programs and procedures of even the most narrow and conservative graduate faculties.

Anyone, however, who is familiar with the slow processes of change in the academic world, anyone who has watched the careers of educational reformers attempting to develop and apply the technique of academic revolution, anyone who has been impressed by the overwhelming inertia and smug self-satisfaction of the academic mind and by the dead weight of departmental vested interests, may well feel that the reform of American graduate education is a divine event, so far off as to encourage despair instead of hope.

What one would like to see is the establishment by some energetic small academic college of a humanistic graduate school planned and operated on almost completely novel lines. Such a graduate school could start without the handicaps of the traditional historical methods and could devote itself to training students, not to become specialists in English, philosophy, music, or the fine arts, but to become

* Even into the graduate school, the light is slowly penetrating. Even Harvard, which, more than any other American institution, has been responsible for the debilitation of humanistic studies through its devotion to the historical-scientific method and the prestige (not altogether deserved) of its degree, has seen the error of its ways, has thrown down many of the linguistic hurdles which protected its graduate students from the fair fields of *belles-lettres*, and now encourages its students to study the relationships between literature and philosophy, or literature and history. And the University of Chicago, which in its earlier days hewed close to the lines laid down by Harvard, has now broken over those lines, and, in the Department of English at any rate, now gives both undergraduates and graduate students perhaps the most broadly conceived, if narrowly considered, training available in the United States.

144

oriented in all the aspects of a particular culture and skilled in interpreting the relationships between those aspects. Fundamental to such a school or institute would be training, not merely in the scientific-historical method of studying the humanities, but equally in the systematic, analytical, and critical methods of studying these subjects. Traditionalists will at once object that such a training would result in breadth, perhaps, but not in depth, but there is no reason why this should be the result. Indeed, it may well be argued that a graduate student who devoted three years to studying the Renaissance or the Victorian era would have not only a depth but a breadth unlike that attained except by a very few absolutely first-rate scholars and critics. There is, moreover, something exceedingly specious about the depth which is the alleged goal of traditional graduate training. At best, most graduate students are not likely to devote more than a year or so to the "special field" in which their dissertations are produced. The rest of such students' time is engaged in getting a more or less superficial knowledge of the whole subject matter of their general field. The "depth" achieved is chronological rather than intellectual. It seems unquestionable that a graduate student trained in various approaches to all the aspects of the Renaissance would have a deeper knowledge than a student who devotes half his time to getting up a field that may cover centuries, a quarter of his time to orienting himself in his "period," and the remainder of his time to writing a dissertation on a hole-in-the-corner subject in his period.

It might indeed be urged that such an institute might initiate its program by limiting its faculty and its students to the study of some major period in human culture. Not only would such an institute be less expensive to organize and operate than a graduate school that attempts to cover every period and field in the humanities, but it would be easier to organize since its objectives could be defined more easily and more easily kept clear. Moreover, the productions of such an institute would set a standard for investigation and scholarly achievement that would rapidly put to shame the productions of the conventional graduate school by their breadth, subtlety, richness, and significance.

But if such an institute is no more than wishful thinking, there is no reason why more modest schemes for the encouragement of a genuinely humanistic approach to humanistic studies should not be launched. The problem of the individual or group or foundation interested in revitalizing the humanities is twofold: that of discovering and encouraging genuine humanists and that of bringing them together. Professor Ducasse has said rightly that "The only place where two subjects can be brought into organic contact and fertilize each other is not a building but a head— the head of a man who is a specialist in one of them and who has an interest in, and some substantial knowledge of, the other." *

In the long run, foundations interested in the humanities could perhaps render no more signal service to humanistic education than by the making of grants-in-aid to persons such as Professor Ducasse has described. They might select men with such interests and give them an opportunity through study and writing to extend their knowledge of some field related to their own and to work out and build up connections between the two fields. Within the space of a year, such men, well grounded in a single subject, could acquire a sufficient grasp of another and related subject to deepen their own intellectual perspective and to enrich their own study and teaching. Men already possessed of vigorous interests in two or more fields might very well carry through some problem in interrelationship with sat-

* C. J. Ducasse, "The Place of Philosophy in General Education" (Unpublished manuscript), p. 81.

isfactory and suggestive results. Such men should, I believe, be either persons who have taken the doctoral degree without any real damage to their vitality and range of interests, or mature men who have not taken the degree and who have proved themselves to be vigorous and stimulating teachers.

Persons concerned with the revival of the humanities might very well encourage, not merely the production of isolated humanists but also the association of such humanists over a more or less extended period. Two types of such association suggest themselves. The first is the interchange between college faculties of their most vital and vigorous members. Such an interchange need not have the formality nor the expense involved in what we have come to call exchange professorships. What I have in mind is something much more informal and inexpensive. At present, there is no more striking feature of small college behavior than its intellectual isolation from other small colleges. Not only are such faculties woefully ignorant of what is going on in higher education generally in the way of developing a new philosophy and new methods of education, but such faculties are generally hostile to such innovations as may come to their attention and smugly satisfied with an uncritical pursuit of familiar procedures. They are also very likely to depend on defense mechanisms to convince themselves that their objectives and procedures are superior to those of the small colleges of their own class and in their own neighborhood. It should be a very simple matter for a group of such small colleges to arrange to exchange—for periods of a fortnight, perhaps—its most vigorous and effective men in some one or other subject in the humanities. Such visitors could not only conduct classes in their own subjects and perhaps give an informal public lecture, but meet with department members and majors in the department for the presentation of the visitor's point of view and interests and a discussion of these matters.

If, however, even this technique of intellectual interchange should seem too complicated, there is every reason why humanists should encourage, within the walls of a single college, a kind of intellectual co-operation now almost nonexistent. It is shocking to discover that in most small colleges and some universities there is almost no intellectual interchange among the members of a single department and even less among members of different but really allied departments. If the small college would throw off the incubus of its assumed duty of teaching its students all there is to know about a single subject and of preparing its more brilliant students for the conventional graduate school, the small liberal arts college, privately endowed, is the ideal location, and ought to be the fertilizing center for intellectual co-operation and educational experimentation. If faculty members find it uncomfortable to discuss serious intellectual problems privately, they might be encouraged to discuss them, at least in the publicity of the classroom. At the moment, the academic classroom is one of the most private places in the world.[18] But there is certainly a distinction between invading a classroom to evaluate practices and sharing a classroom with another colleague willing to take part in a pooling of intellectual resources. The latter arrangement is one that should appeal to any except the most self-conscious and psychologically insecure academic types. Single courses or seminars or discussion groups might easily and inexpensively be initiated in which the habit of genuine intellectual co-operation could be fostered.

The setting forth of such schemes and devices for the revitalizing of the humanities may seem impertinent and gratuitous in a period when humanistic education would seem to be receiving its death-blow through the draining off from the colleges and universities of most of the men and many of the women students by the demands of the armed services of the United States. It may seem even more preposterous to defend and maintain the importance of the humanities at a time when the administrative leaders of some of our colleges and universities have abandoned liberal education, not merely without any serious struggle but with an alacrity in such abandonment that would seem cynical if it were not almost certainly ignorant. The presidents of our great universities—almost without exception—have not only hastened to demonstrate their patriotism and loyalty by using devious recruiting methods upon their own student bodies but have thrown themselves sacrificially under the juggernaut of the Army and Navy.*

But despite the recent betrayal of the academic intellectual by his appointed leaders, despite the almost overwhelming difficulties that face the humanities in a technological society seemingly animated by the will-to-death and bent on destroying itself through technological warfare, the plight of the humanities is not utterly desperate. Of the hundreds of colleges and universities in the United States, much less than a majority have been taken over, in large part, by any one of the armed services. Of the remaining number, many, doubtless, will succumb and die as the lifeblood is drawn from their veins. All of these academic demises will be pathetic; some of them will, in the long run, be favorable to the development of higher education in the United States, since it is obvious that there are many weak and struggling institutions that are "better dead." A few of

* Possibly the sacrifice is less disinterested than it at first appears. College and university presidents, as I have pointed out, are primarily business agents of the boards of trustees and not primarily educators, as they are commonly assumed to be. And as business agents they may be keeping the college going by renting out the plant instead of devoting themselves to keeping liberal education going by making every effort to keep it alive and flourishing.

these academic demises will be tragic, but they will be only incidents in a tragedy of world proportions. Many academic institutions will come through the ordeal. For these it is all important, not only to keep their faith but to know the faith they keep.

Apologists for war are in the habit of saying that some good comes out of it. Without subscribing to this unsavory doctrine, one can see that, if the American colleges and universities are sufficiently alert, the war gives an opportunity for a searching scrutiny of the aims and purposes of higher education, for free and earnest experimentation with programs and pedagogical methods, and for a general putting in order of the humanistic house. The values to the preservation of which the humanities are dedicated are not material or technological; they are intellectual, esthetic, and moral. It is not perhaps pure imagination to conceive of the colleges that manage to survive as foci of a vital human culture, of which the major function will be the preservation of the highest possible values in a world that more than ever before in history threatens their destruction.

There *is* a saving remnant, and that saving remnant is likely to be found where the humanistic teacher gathers a few students about him, and imparts to them the wisdom he has acquired, opens their eyes to the beauty in which the arts are infinitely rich, and deepens their faith in the intrinsic value of the good.

A student, arrogant with youth and strength, is said to have asked his professor what he was going to do to preserve civilization. The professor answered—with perhaps ill-concealed self-satisfaction—"*I* am the civilization that you are fighting to preserve." He would have been a wiser man if he had said, "*You* are the civilization I am attempting to preserve." The war gods may grant us a pitifully small number of students to civilize, but so long as there are a few, the outlook for the humanities is not dark.

END-NOTES

CHAPTER I

The following classification indicates the variety of courses included in liberal arts programs:

1. "*Professional* (education, medicine, law, dentistry, pharmacy, nursing, and veterinary medicine); *vocational* (agriculture, home economics, forestry, fine arts, music, arts, architecture, business and commerce, religion, journalism, library science, and physical education); and *technical* (engineering, mining, and military science)." Evelyn Truth Bixler, *A study of electives in the liberal arts colleges of certain universities in forty-two states* (M.A. thesis, University of Maryland, 1933), quoted in R. Freeman Butts, *The college charts its course* (McGraw-Hill, 1933), p. 266 n.

2. "Today the American university revolves about three structural arrangements: (1) the coexistence of undergraduate, graduate, and professional colleges and schools on the same campus under the corporate control of the university, (2) the supremacy of the *graduate* school of arts and sciences and its recognition as the apex of the university program, and (3) the relegation of the *undergraduate college* of arts and sciences to a place of secondary importance in the total university program." W. H. Cowley, *The large place of the small college* (an address delivered at the seventy-seventh convocation of the University of the State of New York, October 17, 1941), p. 7.

3. "State university colleges of arts and sciences are predominantly giving their attention to students who are registered for two years only and who are chiefly interested in jumping the hurdles of the university professional schools which usually require two years of general education for matriculation. Such students are seldom honest-to-goodness liberal arts undergraduates. They are going through prescribed paces and only a small percentage of them are in search of the intellectual and social breadth which constitutes the chief objective of a general education." *Ibid.*, pp. 9-10.

4. The anthropologist, Margaret Mead, finds the roots of the American passion for success in the typical pattern of American family history. "Most of us are third-generation Americans. Grandfather did his best to leave the Old Country behind him, to train Father to be an American . . . The third generation is conscious of having a grandfather who sought liberty in a new country, but his picture of that 'epic' is dulled by the fact that Father does not respect the old man. It is his simple duty to outstrip the father. Thus begins . . . the typical American race for success. Success, not class, . . . is the American

standard of a man's value, rooted deeply in the Puritan belief that toil and struggle are the proper works of man. 'In his parents' every gesture, the child learns that although they want to love him very much . . . they are not quite sure that he will deserve it . . .' Thus, from the first, a child must struggle in competition if he is to be loved and respected." *Time*, November 30, 1942, pp. 106, 108 (a review of Miss Mead's *And keep your powder dry*, Morrow, 1942).

5. The measurement of an American's success in terms of his acquisition of possessions is aided and abetted by what Miss Mead regards as his strongest point, "an exceptional power of analysis, coupled with exceptional ingenuity. The American has no rival at analyzing, not substances, but operational methods, identifying and eliminating lost motion and distinguishing the effective from the useless . . . The most spectacular demonstration of this quality is to be found in our mechanical equipment, admittedly the finest in the world and by long odds." New York *Herald Tribune Books*, November 22, 1942, p. 1 (a review of Miss Mead's book, *And keep your powder dry*).

6. A more formal and authoritative statement of the scientific method is that of W. C. Dampier-Whetham in the *Encyclopædia Britannica*, Fourteenth Edition, Vol. XX, p. 121. "The multitude of phenomena are too great for any subject which aims at explanation and not only at description to be attacked with success without the aid of hypothesis framed by the use of the scientific imagination. Facts are collected to prove or disprove the consequences deduced from the hypothesis, and thus the number of facts to be examined becomes manageable. If agreement is found, the hypothesis is, so far, confirmed, and gains in authority with every fresh concordance discovered. If the deductions from the hypothesis do not agree with the accepted interpretation of facts, the hypothesis may need modification, it may have to be abandoned altogether, or the want of concordance may point to some error or inconsistency in the fundamental concepts on which the hypothesis is based—the whole framework of that branch of science may need revision."

For a fuller exposition of the complexities of the scientific method, see Abraham Wolf's article on "Scientific Method," *ibid.*, XX, 127-33.

Of the limited applicability of the scientific method, even to the field of the social sciences, Dr. Irving Langmuir, retiring President of the A.A.A.S., says, "I can see no justification whatever for such teaching that science proves that general causes (convergent phenomena) dominate in human affairs over the results of individual action (divergent phenomena)." . . . Dividing natural phenomena into two types, Dr. Langmuir cited one kind in which the behavior of a system can be determined from the average behavior of its various parts. Those he called "convergent phenomena." The second group he classified as "divergent phenomena," in which a single predictable event becomes magnified in its effect "so that the behavior of the whole aggregate does depend upon something that started from a small beginning . . . Human affairs are characterized by a complexity of a far higher order than that encountered ordinarily in the field of science . . . I believe the

152

field of application of science in such problems is extremely limited." New York *Times*, December 27, 1942, p. 31.

7. Tucker Brooke's *Shakespeare of Stratford* (Yale University Press, 1926) is a convenient illustration of the abyss between the objective and the subjective approach to a highly problematical character. In the body of this volume, Professor Brooke has assembled all the objective evidence concerning his subject's passage through this mortal world. In a brilliant essay, which he assigns to an appendix, he indicates what on the basis of the objective evidence *and* of the works, he believes the man Shakespeare to have been. Students who believe that objective evidence is adequate to the solution of literary problems might very well attempt to arrive at some conclusion as to the character of Shakespeare by limiting their attention to the objective material in this handy volume.

8. Another striking example of the distinction between the objective and the subjective treatment of literary materials is offered by Caroline E. Spurgeon's *Shakespeare's imagery and what it tells us* (Cambridge University Press, 1935). The patient accumulation and classification of Shakespeare's imagery was a predominantly objective task. The interpretation of Shakespeare's character on the basis of the number and weight of his images required powers of intuition and insight the writer did not bring to her task. A critic summarizing Miss Spurgeon's conclusions writes, "Miss Spurgeon's picture is of a man keenly sensitive to all sights and sounds, quietly observant of the thronging crowds around him, deeply imbued with a love of nature and, above all, intensely conscious of everything in life which possessed movement." Allardyce Nicoll, *Year's work in English studies* (1937), Vol. XVI, p. 175. Shakespeare may have been the tepid, genteel nature-lover these words suggest, but one doubts it.

9. "Under the same 'scientific' impulse, literature was dissected and picked to pieces like a beetle in a laboratory. The social sciences lost their humanity in a false scientism that tended to make them sterile. After years of substituting information for wisdom, the Regents Inquiry finally made the amazing but obvious discovery that possession of facts supplies neither the incentive nor the direction for their proper use. Facts and values belong in different realms. It would be amusing, if it were not tragic, to realize that a period which laid so much emphasis upon relevance of materials laid so little upon relevance of method in studying those materials. It has long been clear that science has a great part to play in liberal education. But it should be equally clear that it must play its role directly, not by imposing its characteristics upon other disciplines whose methods and results, equally valid, are simply different." T. M. Greene, *et al.*, *Liberal education re-examined; its role in a democracy* (Harper, 1943), p. 13.

10. "Albert Feuillerat . . . in a suggestive article entitled 'Scholarship and Literary Criticism' . . . welcomed the scientific method of the nineteenth century as a corrective of mere subjectivism, but deplored the degeneration of it into a pedantry that converted the means into an end, that accumulated facts without regard for any purpose beyond them. In divorcing itself from literary criticism, scholarship had be-

153

trayed the cause of literature in the American college, had abandoned the ambition of 'playing a part in the education of the nation at large,' and thus had divorced itself from the public as well. 'Let us frankly acknowledge,' he proposed, 'that we have made a mistake. When the twentieth century began, two ways were open to us. One of them prolonged in a straight line the beaten trail; the other diverged. By some error on our part we took the oblique way, and now it has proved to be a blind alley. . . . Let us therefore retrace our steps to the crossroads where scholarship and critcism began to separate.' " Norman Foerster, "The study of letters," in *Literary scholarship, its aims and methods* (University of North Carolina Press, 1941), pp. 14-15.

11. "When knowledge is thus cut up into little segments and administered to students in unrelated fragments, it loses significance and vitality and fails to appeal to the interests of youth, because it seems so far removed from the problems of life, the solution of which calls for the breadth of knowledge and the depth of understanding which go beyond the artificial boundaries between subjects and departments. It is true that the whole field of knowledge is so vast that it is necessary for the purposes of study to divide it into sections, examining each at a time. The trouble is that, in the present status of rigid departmental organization, the sections are never put together again and the students are not given definite help to organize the parts into intelligible wholes." T. H-E. Chen, *Developing patterns of the college curriculum in the United States*, "Southern California Education Monographs, No. 10" (University of Southern California Press, 1940), p. 10.

12. "Institutions dedicated to humanism perpetually develop agencies which thwart this purpose. There are four such dehumanizing influences that may be singled out for special mention—technique, the multiplication of accessory disciplines, departmental separation, and vocational utility. Technique tends to become a game played for its own sake. It tends to divorce expertness from significance, and thus to trivialize research and blind both student and teacher to the purposes by which technique is justified. Owing to the extension of knowledge, the cult of thoroughness and precision, and the intellectual division of labor, 'there is,' to quote Professor Dodds, 'a continual hiving off of specialists from the central swarm.' [E. R. Dodds, *Humanism and technique in Greek studies*, Inaugural lecture as Regius Professor, Oxford, 1936, p. 6.] This multiplication of more or less autonomous entities is aggravated by the artificial barriers of academic departments, created for administrative purposes, but profoundly affecting the intellectual life of those who live *within* them. Finally, since the teacher has his job, and the student hopes to find one, it is inevitable that both should have an eye to the market for their wares. The teachers of the present era have been affected by all of these tendencies. All teachers were, during the most formative period, students. They are products of the system which is now entrusted to their keeping. They have been reared in laboratories, classrooms, and departments, where they have become habituated to some specialized procedure, and where they have looked upon their acquisitions as the tools of a trade. I do not say that these tendencies are either preventable or undesirable. But in some degree they militate

154

against the teacher's realizing those humane possibilities which his subject, whatever it is, possesses." R. B. Perry, "A definition of the humanities," in *The meaning of the humanities* (Princeton University Press, 1938), p. 33.

13. "Narrow specialization in the college is re-enforced by the system of departmentalization and the tradition of departmental autonomy in college administration. . . . College professors are so concerned with the development of their respective departments that they fail to see the program of the college as a whole. Specialization isolates them from other departments, on the one hand, and from the vital issues of life, on the other. Says Richardson: 'Too many college teachers are not really interested in the vital problems of the college. Each is keenly interested in his own department. . . . His live interest, when matters of curriculum are considered, is to see that his department shall not suffer. We go largely on the absurd principle that an effective unified college can be built by the maximum development of individual departments, each proceeding on its way without much regard to another.' " [L. B. Richardson, *A study of the liberal college* (Dartmouth College, 1924), p. 261.] Chen, *op. cit.,* p. 9.

14. "The 'unbelievably picayunish' features of doctoral dissertations that satirists have ridiculed are not so much a deliberate choice on the part of candidates as of numerous pressures brought to bear upon them. Professors often set capable students to trivial and minutely specialized tasks to fill in the gaps in their own larger studies, or the candidate himself may pick a narrow topic of relatively little import in order to get positive results in a limited time. Already beset by a mild anxiety neurosis as foreshortened time becomes a more precious commodity, the thesis writer is realistically reluctant to attempt 'great heroic work with large risks and possibilities of infinite delay.' These pressures are generated by an academic ideology (widely shared) that tends to measure the worth of a study by its precision rather than its importance. Aping the physical scientists, social scientists do homage to the third decimal point of exactitude. Particularly flagrant in the humanities is the field of English, where the philologists rather than the broad scholars have been in the saddle. According to one authority, the situation is in no small part due to the failure of the humanists to provide young scholars with acceptable problems, whereas those scholars with a highly specialized view of research are full of problems and stereotyped procedures." Logan Wilson, *The academic man* (Oxford University Press, 1942), pp. 43-44.

15. "The man who knows his subject; who in addition has obtained in its realm information which was not known before; such a man is competent to teach that subject at any place, at any time, to any group. Such is the theory which governs the training in the graduate school, as far as it works on any conscious theory at all. No one will dispute the fundamental necessity of knowing on the part of the man who is to induce others to know, and no one would advocate a change which would affect deleteriously this element of the student's preparation. But to say that this element is the sole one to be considered, is to say something which is palpably untrue. The college teacher who knows

well a narrow field, but who knows not how to impart that knowledge to others, who is ignorant of other fields and of the relationship of his subject to them, who has never grasped the idea of the unity of knowledge, whose intellectual curiosity is bounded within narrow limits, whose appreciation of a wide range of intellectual enjoyments has never been aroused; that man will never be effective in his chosen work. But such a product may well be produced by the graduate school, for all the institution consciously does to prevent that result." Leon B. Richardson, *A study of the liberal college* (a report to the president of Dartmouth College, 1924), p. 266.

CHAPTER II

1. The following principles have been suggested as criteria for judging any curriculum organization. "The organization of a curriculum should be such that: 1. Students will gain a comprehensive understanding of the fields they study. 2. Students will make contact with the frontiers of knowledge and see it as a growing thing. 3. Students will accept a high degree of responsibility for their own education. 4. Both students and faculty will be stimulated to sound scholarship." Melvin E. Haggerty, *The evaluation of higher institutions*, a series of monographs, Vol. III. "The Educational Problem" (The University of Chicago Press), pp. 208-09.

2. R. Freeman Butts has classified recent educational experiments as follows:

"I. Administrative shuffling of course requirements
    A. Concentration and distribution
    B. Majors and minors
    C. Group system
II. Individualized instruction
    A. Tutorial and preceptorial plans
    B. Honors and independent study plans
    C. Reading periods and flexible attendance requirements
    D. Individual conferences, discussion groups, and seminars
    E. Field activities
    F. House plans
    G. Student interests and experiences as a starting point
III. Greater prescription to increase integration and afford common funds of knowledge
    A. Broader fields of knowledge
    B. Comprehensive examinations
    C. Survey courses
    D. Culture epochs and needs of living
    E. Prescribed books."

For a discussion of these experiments, see Professor Butts's *The college charts its course* (McGraw-Hill, 1939), pp. 409-15. Most of the procedures listed under III are discussed in this chapter and most of the pedagogical procedures listed under II are considered in Chapter III of this survey.

3. "Investigation and analysis have led the author to distinguish six different patterns of the curriculum which are developing in colleges and universities active in experimenting with new ways of curriculum organization. These six patterns are:

"1. A curriculum marked by the introduction of instructional methods and devices designed to break down the lock-step system of credits, formal lectures, and the mechanization of education. Conspicuous among such methods and devices are the tutorial or honors plans for the encouragement of independent study and the institution of comprehensive examinations to shift the emphasis from credit accumulation and timeserving to organized knowledge within a field.

"2. A curriculum marked by efforts to avoid narrow specialization and rigid departmentalization. The effort may be no more than a mere administrative grouping of departments into divisions, involving no integration of departmentalized subject matter and producing, in effect, no real change in the essential nature of the curriculum. Or, further steps may be taken toward the fusion or integration of subject matter in interdepartmental courses of various types.

"3. A curriculum of classical studies and 'great books' of the ages. The central aim is the revival of the liberal arts and the traditional disciplines of the medieval university.

"4. A curriculum organized around a few major fields of knowledge or human achievement, with a core of general interdepartmental courses representing the required minimum of general education. The judgment of the faculty and of experts representing different fields provides the criteria which guide the determination of the major fields or areas and the organization of courses for the different fields or areas.

"5. A curriculum built upon the major functions of modern living determined by a survey of the activities and needs of students and of alumni in active careers. The survey data, interpreted and evaluated in the light of a philosophy of general education in the present age, provide the basis not only for the determination of the major areas of living but also for the organization of course content for each of the areas.

"6. A curriculum based upon the interests, abilities, and needs of each individual student. The interests and needs of the student are discovered not by any survey of groups of students but by the intimate personal knowledge of each individual student. The curriculum is individually planned. Individual education replaces mass education; personal arrangements take the place of general requirements and standards; informal flexible methods supplant the machinery of quantitative education." Chen, *op. cit.*, p. 19.

4. "The organization of higher learning by subject-matter departments . . . has been widely condemned for various shortcomings. That it produces anarchic effects such as the duplication of efforts, lack of planning and coordination, minimization of outside contacts and mutual interaction, a dispersal of effort and pottering away at isolated problems

has often been pointed out. However necessary such an intellectual division of labor, it inadvertently creates staff tensions within the university, and often has some of the following results:

" '1. Rivalry between the various departments in securing students for their classes, by appealing either to administrative organization which decides upon required portions of the curriculum or to the students themselves who decide upon elective courses at the registration period.

" '2. Rivalry between departments in securing administrative favor in the apportionment of funds for maintenance and expansion, or in the effort to enhance their academic prestige in the institution as a whole.

" '3. The narrowing of the interests and activities of the members of a department to problems wholly related to the development of the subject of that department.

" '4. The sharpening of the lines of specialized knowledge for the student—the building of tightly compartmented units in the education of the student.' " [James S. Kinder, *The internal administration of the liberal arts college* (Teachers College, Columbia University, 1934), pp. 133-134.] Wilson, *op. cit.*, p. 83.

5. For some time, Harvard University has offered interdepartmental Honors programs in Literature, History and Literature, and History and Science. As an example of these programs, the following statement of the requirements for Honors work in History and Literature may be quoted: "A student concentrating in History and Literature must take at least six courses (not more than two of which are regularly open to freshmen) so selected as to come under some general scheme of study of the History and Literature either of a nation or of a period: for example—the History and Literature (a) of Greece, (b) of England, (c) of France; the History and Literature (d) of the Middle Ages, (e) of the Renaissance, (f) of the Nineteenth Century . . . The student will normally be expected to divide his work about equally between courses in Literature and courses in History. In addition, he will pursue a course of general reading both in the principal authors of the country or of the period in question and in the works of standard authorities concerning these matters. Each student is required to have a knowledge of eight books of the Bible (any standard version, ancient or modern, may be used), and of eight plays of Shakespeare. This knowledge will be tested in written examinations at the end of the Sophomore year. In addition, each student concentrating in the Modern field is expected to make himself thoroughly familiar with the works of one ancient historian and of one ancient author not an historian; each concentrator in the Ancient field is expected to pursue a similar course of study in connection with a modern historian and a modern author not an historian. Students will be given an examination to test this knowledge at the beginning of the Junior year." "Rules Relating to College Studies," *Official Register of Harvard University* (1939), Vol. 36, No. 8, p. 26. For further details concerning the History and Literature Honors program and the program in Literature, and in History and Science, see the same official announcement.

6. "In his inaugural address, Lowell later indicated that he would proceed to limit further the free elective system by requiring the stu-

dent to specialize more thoroughly in one field and at the same time to take a certain amount of work in each of several other fields. Consequently, in 1910, Harvard's famous plan of 'concentration and distribution' went into effect, whereby all undergraduate subjects were classified into four large fields: arts of expression (language, literature, fine arts, and music); natural sciences; social sciences; and mathematics and philosophy. In order to provide for concentration, the student was required to take at least six of his sixteen elective courses within one of these divisions; and to provide for distribution, he must divide another six courses among the three remaining fields. In this way, Lowell and his committee hoped that students' choices would secure for them a more systematic education, based upon the principle that a liberally educated person should know a little of everything and something well. Lowell also aimed to encourage students to plan their courses seriously and to plan them as a whole. With this change in the policy of Harvard, which had supported so long and so strongly the principle of free election under President Eliot, a definite phase in the history of the elective system appeared to be ended." Butts, *op. cit.*, pp. 246-47.

7. "The present tendency to organize general academic knowledge for early college years in a few broad fields requiring an examination for each, has peculiar advantages . . . It fixes an impressive provisional aim that is unmistakably educational, namely, to review in a constructive, related fashion the essentials of organized knowledge. As a curriculum this appears rigid; yet, if well administered without course-credits but with skilled teachers and good examinations, it is completely flexible. For minds whose ultimate purposes are partly or wholly defined, it offers every opportunity for rapid advance with whatever emphases are most desired. For those whose final aims are uncertain, it lays out for inspection the significant values in all fields and makes possible an informed and deliberate choice.

"Under such an arrangement as a vestibule to final concentration, a student may advantageously spend a large share of his course in defining his ultimate aim, but the college sees to it that he has a clear purpose, and that every stroke he takes counts toward focusing his permanent intellectual interest." Wm. S. Learned and B. D. Wood, *The student and his knowledge* (The Carnegie Foundation for the Advancement of Teaching, 1938), p. 51.

8. The texts thus far published by Harper and Brothers are *Experience, reason, and faith*, by E. G. Bewkes and others; *Men, groups, and the community*, by T. H. Robinson and others; *The human organism and the world of life*, by C. W. Young and others; and *Atoms, rocks, and galaxies*, by J. S. Allen and others. The text for the fifth survey in fine arts and literature is being prepared by Professors J. F. Fitchin and Alfred Krakusin.

9. "One of the most serious difficulties (in the operation of interdepartmental courses) is the dearth of broadly trained teachers who are themselves able to see the interrelationships of knowledge and have the creative ability to organize content along lines different from those to which they have become accustomed. The success of the interdepartmental courses is proportional to the ability of the instructors to

159

synthesize knowledge from different departments and to see the broad relations of subjects to one another and to the vital issues of contemporary life.

"Possible advantages of well-organized inter-departmental courses may be summed up as follows:

"1. They emphasize the interrelationship of departments.

"2. They point a way toward the synthesis of knowledge.

"3. They meet the needs of the layman and the citizen rather than of the scholar. They serve the purpose of general education.

"4. They are not a substitute for detailed knowledge of the traditional courses, but provide a background for deeper understanding. They enable students 'to ascend to the mountain top and to survey the promised land before they go down to occupy it.' [H. E. Hawkes, *Five college plans* (Columbia University Press, 1931), p. 23.]

"5. They help the student to discover his interests, thus leading to a more intelligent choice of a field of concentration.

"6. They make possible the direct study of realistic life problems, the understanding of which requires the integration of knowledge from different academic fields." Chen, *op. cit.*, p. 65.

10. In the new "four-year" College at Chicago, there has been no significant modification of the weighting apparent in the earlier program there. In the new program, three-year courses in each of the four areas: Humanities, Biological Sciences, Physical Sciences, and Social Sciences, are now offered. The organization of the three-year course in the Humanities is perhaps of sufficient interest to warrant the insertion of its official description:

"The three-year sequence of courses in the humanities deals with literature, art, music, philosophy, and history. Its purpose is to acquaint students with the major achievements in these fields and to develop competence in the analysis, understanding, and appreciation of historical, rhetorical, literary, and philosophic writings and of works of art and music. The three courses which make up the series deal progressively with richer and more difficult materials and aim at increasing progressively the ability of students to use the humanistic disciplines and skills.

"*Humanities 1.* An introduction to literature, art, and music. Three of the five class meetings each week are given to discussion of the novels, plays, and poems which comprise the readings listed in the syllabus for the course. These discussions are devoted to training students in the art of reading so as to lay the foundations for a sensitive and intelligent understanding and enjoyment of literature. The other two class sessions each week are given to art and music, the former during the first half, the latter during the second half of the year. The work in art is based upon illustrated lectures, readings in the history of art, visits to the University's Art Reference Library, tours of galleries, and discussions of paintings, architecture, and sculpture. The work in music is conducted by lectures, reading, and discussions based upon a carefully arranged schedule of musical reproductions. As in the study of literature, the study of art and music is designed to provide the basis for sensitive and intelligent appreciation . . .

"*Humanities 2.* A course is devoted to history and literature. During the first part of the year students read a number of great histories, and throughout the year they attend lectures given once a week by members of the University faculty engaged in historical research, who explain the nature of their problems and present the results of their work on them. The reading of histories during the first part of the year is followed by the reading of dramatic literature and works of fiction. The readings on the list are fewer in number and considerably more difficult than those of the first year. The emphasis during this year is placed upon the arts of interpretation needed for the full understanding of historical, rhetorical, dramatic, and fictional works. Students meet three times each week in small discussion sections which are devoted to training in careful analysis and proper appreciation of the books read . . .

"*Humanities 3.* A course devoted to lyric poetry, philosophy, art, and music. The emphasis during this year is placed upon the theoretic side of humanistic study. Besides practical training in the arts required for understanding and appreciating poetry, philosophy, art, and music, the work is turned to the study of the theories which have been used to explain the origin, nature, and effect of the humanistic works." "The College and the Divisions for Sessions of 1943-44," *The University of Chicago Announcements,* pp. 55-56.

11. The program of St. John's College represents, of course, the extremist development of the attempt to give students a common core of intellectual experience. Under this system, as I understand it, practically all the work of the four-year course is taken by all the students in the college. The core of the program is the series of "great books"—classics in philosophy, religion, literature, and science—which serve to introduce the student to the intellectual and cultural history of western man. "The purpose of the new curriculum is the cultivation of the intellect by means of the study of the liberal arts. The liberal arts are 'the arts of apprehending, understanding, and knowing.' [*Catalogue of St. John's College,* 1937-38, p. 21.] 'The clearest historic pattern of the liberal arts for the modern mind is . . . to be found in the thirteenth century.' [*Ibid.,* p. 28.] They consist of the *trivium,* viz., grammar, rhetoric, and logic; and the *quadrivium,* viz., arithmetic, geometry, music, and astronomy. For the study of these arts, a list of more than a hundred 'great books' is selected. 'The entire period with the books and the patterns of the arts can be recapitulated in the four-year college course, the yearly divisions falling, respectively, at the end of the Alexandrian period, at the end of the Middle Ages, in the middle of the eighteenth century, and ending with contemporary writers.' [*Ibid.,* p. 29.]" Chen, *op. cit.,* pp. 69-70.

CHAPTER III

1. "But while we assign the lecture its due place in the college system, if we attempt to carry it farther and to make the real teaching of the American student depend upon this method of instruction, we shall

encounter definite and unmistakable failure. It simply will not work. It never does work even in those institutions which most stress it. If anyone doubts this statement, let him select that lecturer among his colleagues whom he considers most able, let him sit among the students in his courses and observe the reaction of really effective lecturing upon them. He will find on the part of most a real interest. But it is a passive rather than an active interest. Many make no attempt to take notes at all; those who do, in many cases, achieve marked success in noting non-essentials at the expense of things really important, and unbelievable ingenuity in perverting the sense of what is said to a meaning often exactly opposite that intended. The only way in which a lecturer can be sure that a point which he wishes to make shall be noted by a majority of his students is to say that it will probably be on the examination: a process utterly absurd as a method of education, and one which leads some students to put it down right, and some to put it down wrong, and some to put it down not at all, but to rely on somebody else to do so for them." Richardson, *op. cit.*, pp. 194-95.

2. "To some teachers it is a most attractive idea that they can simply talk and talk with no interruption from anyone; with no necessity of concerning themselves with the difficulties of individuals, and with no chance that a smoothly working schedule by which they calculate that they may 'cover the course' may, in any way, be impeded. A teacher of this type is usually conscientious enough in the performance of his duties; he toils without rest over his material, he endeavors to assemble it in the best possible form and to deliver it in the best possible way. When he has acquired, by experience, an idea of the method by which these things may effectively be done; and when, in addition, he acquires some notion of the average scale of intelligence of the men under him, so that he will not shoot too high or too low, he may become a good lecturer—or he may not. It is really surprising how many men of the latter type—some of them men of long experience—are lecturing in our colleges." Richardson, *op. cit.*, p. 193.

3. W. S. Learned and B. D. Wood, *The student and his knowledge* (The Carnegie Foundation for the Advancement of Teaching, 1937), p. 21. The scores of college seniors who were planning to become teachers produced the most shocking findings of the survey: "The results concern two large groups of prospective teachers about to graduate from college—1,422 out of a total of 4,412 students tested in 1928, and 1,410 out of a total of 2,280 tested in 1932. In both tests the teachers' average was below the total score for the entire group and was below all other group averages except those of the business, art, agriculture, and secretarial candidates. In the second test, the artists scored above the teachers." *Ibid.*, pp. 38-39. "The median score of the teachers is 626. Above this are the scores of 12 per cent of the high-school seniors; 22 per cent of them have scores above 25 per cent of the teachers. Seven per cent of the prospective teachers make lower scores than 36 per cent of the high-school pupils. Thirteen per cent of the high-school participants score higher than 44 per cent of the college group." *Ibid.*, p. 41.

4. At Harvard, the General Examination required of candidates in

the ancient and modern language departments is either a purely general or a combined general and departmental examination. This General Examination is taken at the end of the student's junior year. For candidates in the classics, the examination covers the Bible, Shakespeare, and the important works of two of the following modern authors: Dante, Cervantes, Chaucer, Milton, Molière, and Goethe. "The examination on the Bible will call for a knowledge of the subject-matter of ten books or groups of books of the Bible . . . the examination on Shakespeare will be on twelve plays; the modern authors may be read, if necessary in translation." "Rules Relating to College Studies," *Official Register of Harvard University*, Vol. XXXVI, No. 8, p. 19. Every student in a department in one of the modern languages "is required to show (1) a knowledge of the literature in which he concentrates; (2) a knowledge of twelve plays of Shakespeare, of the subject-matter of ten books or groups of books of the Bible . . . and of the important works of two of the following authors: Homer, Sophocles, Plato, Aristotle, Cicero, Horace, Virgil." *Ibid.*, p. 30.

5. "Nevertheless it is probable that the examination as a part of our educational machinery may be made to fulfill its purpose in the scheme of the college more effectively than it now does. It is doubtful if at any point of our present system increased care on the part of the teacher can be made to yield more fruitful results than at this. A process by which the general level of examinations is raised requires time and thought, but both the time and the thought will be found to be well spent.

"Particularly fruitful in their promise are examinations of the new type: those in which the length of answer is reduced to the minimum, in which blanks are filled in, or sentences completed, statements are marked true or false, or the correct answer is selected from a list of possibilities. Such examinations offer many advantages. They are fair; they cover a large amount of material; they require little time in the actual process of writing; and their reliability is a demonstrated fact. They can easily be made tests of reasoning power and of the use of materials. They are generally approved by the students, despite the fact that they constitute much more exacting tests than do examinations of the ordinary type." Richardson, *op. cit.*, p. 210.

6. *History 10, history of Western civilization, a syllabus* (Stanford University, 1941), p. 2. The combination of lectures and discussion groups is normal for survey courses in the Humanities. On this feature, Patricia Beesley writes, "Characteristic also of the majority of Humanities courses is the lecture method of presentation. Lectures are variously designed as brief introductory surveys of a period to be studied intensively, sketches of the political and social background of an important cultural era, discussions of the life and works of a single great figure, analyses of important esthetic principles, etc. Because such lectures are usually delivered to large groups of students, either by one professor or by a number of professors, each presenting the material of his special field, small discussion sections and individual conferences are also employed to assist the student to master the material of the course. . . . Discussion sections and conferences are frequently devoted to the

consideration of . . . assigned reading or to brief quizzes on the material recently covered." *The revival of the humanities in American education* (Columbia University Press, 1940), p. 27.

7. "Different forms of tutorial or honors work and comprehensive examinations, given either at the end or at some other time of the college course, have been widely adopted by colleges and universities over all parts of the country . . . Out of the 168 institutions included in the study reported in the *Thirty-first yearbook of the N.S.S.E.*, more than a hundred institutions were found to have adopted some form of tutorial or honors work. [*Thirty-first yearbook of the N.S.S.E.*, Part II, pp. 33-34.]" T. H-E. Chen, *Developing patterns of the college curriculum in the United States*, "Southern California Education Monographs" (University of Southern California Press, 1940), p. 43.

8. "The student is of more importance than the curriculum. His growth in knowledge and in wisdom is at the core of the educational process. The school should be free to deal with the child as a human being. This the school cannot do so long as it has supreme faith in its own administrative techniques. The intellectual career of the student through the school should be determined not only by his capacity but by his progressive attainment in the field of enduring knowledge. This involves less emphasis upon administrative techniques of the unit-credit type and more emphasis upon the individual student. With the growth of administrative wisdom, tests would not be treated as mere educational gadgets but as tools to be used to free the student in his academic advancement. There has already been wide acceptance of this idea, and, as experience accumulates, many of the obstacles, which are more or less mechanical, will be overcome." Learned and Wood, *op. cit.*, p. xiii.

9. "With the 'average student' disposed of, there remain only individuals. These should command exclusive attention. What they are, what they know, what they can and will learn, are separate, individual problems. When we behave officially as though all pupils and students were alike we deny the student a revelation that lies at the core of all educational reality. If the educational process has any chance whatever of inducing a respect for intellectual honesty and the habit of its practice, this can result only from the truthful and realistic manner in which individual minds are dealt with. There can be few formulas for the purpose; more than in most other services the successful educator must depend on intelligence." *Ibid.*, p. 45.

10. The absurdities to which the system of close supervision of the student's extracurricular behavior may lead are suggested in a passage from an article, "Confessions of a College Dean," written by an anonymous dean of men in a medium-sized American college. "Practically he is a policeman. He must spend substantially all his time promulgating, and, so far as possible, enforcing, the multifarious rules and regulations which the faculty are constantly enacting. Among the things which it is the dean's business to make the student do are the following:

"1. To spend, spasmodically at least, a certain minimum of time in study. 2. To attend classes . . . 3. To attend chapel. 4. To participate in military drill. 5. To take regular physical exercise. 6. To be vaccinated. 7. To refrain from gross cheating in (a) final examinations, (b) mid-semester quizzes, (c) laboratory exercises, and (d) themes, theses, and other written work prepared outside the classroom. 8. To refrain from getting drunk, at least in public. 9. To refrain from smoking in the college buildings. 10. To keep hazing and class scraps within such bounds that actual loss of life or limb will not occur frequently. 11. To omit from the college 'comic' magazine jokes and pictures of such undisguised indecency as would render the publication unmailable under U. S. postal regulations. 12. To close college dances at some specified hour prior to daybreak. 13. To have at least nominal chaperons present at such dances. 14. To pay their bills to the college and the local merchants. 15. To refrain from writing checks with no balance in the bank; also from forgery. 16. To refrain from using automobiles except under certain narrow restrictions. 17. To keep off the grass." *The New Republic*, June 22, 1927, p. 117.

11. "The student should be put upon his own resources more than he now is; he should be placed in the attitude of one who must master a wide field, the material being before him, largely by his own initiative. Formal exercises, as the work develops, should more and more be devoted to the synthesis of the facts gained, to the construction of a logical point of view, to the discussion of the salient features that develop, and less and less to the purpose of finding out what the student knows. Such exercises in themselves are a sufficient test of whether or not he is doing his work, and the individual who is idle should be dropped from that field of concentration, and left as a result with no place to turn. No pretentious spirit of research should invade the course; it is to be planned, not for the professional scholar, but for the intelligent man of the world. Nevertheless the method by which material in such a process must be handled is essentially that of the investigator, although the problem may have been worked upon by others, and the conclusions reached may be far from new. So, while he will be making no 'new contribution to knowledge,' the student will be working in the way in which those who do contribute to knowledge must work, and he will be doing it himself." Richardson, *op. cit.*, p. 177.

12. "From the point of view of the individual, the implications of the experimental position are fully as far-reaching. The conception of *growth* in education resulted in a much greater respect for the individual student and for his development as a unique individuality. Education came to be visualized in terms of the physical, intellectual, emotional, and moral growth of students rather than in terms of the discipline of fixed faculties. Furthermore, the conception of the *active* character of experience proved to be very fruitful for educational theory and techniques. Since experience is the interaction of the organism and environment, then knowing and meaning arise only when there is an active response on the part of the individual. That learning is viewed as best which encourages the learner himself to take the initiative in planning, carrying out, and judging his own activities. Learning is best when students themselves have the freedom to carry out those activities which seem to be in line with their own genuine purposes and interests. The test of learning thus becomes not the ability to recite in class or

write an examination so much as it is the ability to act intelligently in subsequent experiences." Butts, *op. cit.*, p. 277.

13. "The progressive approach to college learning would seem to demand that the newer evidence of science and psychology should be assimilated into the actual practice of learning in college. It would seem to indicate that we should discard conceptions of learning that were formulated before modern science came on to the scene to revise the older notions of intellectual learning. Modern conceptions, of course, do not rule out the importance of learning through books, but they do insist that learning through actual experience is a method which must be given greater attention if college education is to be brought up to date.

"Modern conceptions also insist that the physiological and emotional processes cannot be disregarded in learning; they are integral parts of any learning process adequately conceived. Hence, older conceptions that try to separate the intellectual from bodily functions in accordance with a rationalistic theory of learning must give way to newer conceptions more in line with the best evidence concerning human experience and the development of broader ranges of human personality. This means that a progressive theory of college education would try to reshape the college in such a way that students have more opportunity to develop the broader and deeper reaches of their personalities through social and creative activities of all sorts." Butts, *ibid.*, p. 419.

14. "The fundamental conclusion of this study, therefore, is that each student's self-education should constitute the controlling object of any educational agency that deals with him. In order to endure, an education must be self-achieved. To place this fact in the foreground should make us wary of factitious aids that obscure the simplicity and arduousness of genuine achievement or that weaken a student's responsibility with over-tutelage.

"Schooling organized for self-education will require a design unlike our present procedure. To 'educate' a group of persons in the traditional sense implies emphases that suit chiefly the educator; to stimulate the beneficiary he frequently uses measures of success not closely related to achievement. One who is effectively educating himself is not likely to find such emphases or measures appropriate." Learned and Wood, *op. cit.*, pp. 44-45.

15. René Wellek, "Literary History," in *Literary scholarship: its aims and methods,* by Norman Foerster *et al.* (The University of North Carolina Press, 1941), p. 105.

The great need for training in intensive reading may be graphically illustrated by citing one "false" and one "true" reading of Yeats's poem, "After long silence."

> Speech after long silence; it is right,
> All other lovers being estranged or dead,
> Unfriendly lamplight hid under its shade,
> The curtains drawn upon unfriendly night,
> That we descant and then again descant
> Upon the supreme theme of Art and Song:

166

> Bodily decrepitude is wisdom; young
> We loved each other and were ignorant.

(W. B. Yeats, *Collected Poems*, 1940,
p. 304. Printed by permission of the
Macmillan Company, New York.)

Both readings come from students of very high academic standing.

A. "The poem is concerned with two young people making love in a seductively illuminated room, and herein I believe I have expressed the theme better than did our author. The lovers speak after a long silence; from 'it is right' one gathers that their topic is the question of the morality of their passions, for they 'descant and yet again descant upon the supreme theme of art and song,' namely, 'Bodily decrepitude is wisdom.' All they seemed to know or care about, as young people usually do, was that they loved one another; nothing else entered their minds, the passion of love alone held sway—and they 'were ignorant.' This is like most others a frequent theme for the poet, and the critic must judge the work on its ability to convey its meaning and its expression of the situation. This is where the artist fails; his subject is acceptable, his treatment deplorable. On a poem of this sort it is relatively easy for the critic to pass judgment, for the work expresses an emotional situation which the critic has probably experienced at least to *some* active extent. From his own background, therefore, he can judge if the poem expresses his feelings under the circumstances which the poem presents and in which he (the critic) has personally engaged. I do not believe the poem conveys, as it should, the emotional tension of the two lovers, and I feel that one of the lovers who is supposedly relating this personal experience would not have spoken so unfeelingly after his traumatic experience."

B. "The poem depicts a concrete scene: an elderly man and woman are seated in the evening in a room with a shaded lamp and drawn curtains, simply talking. Perhaps they are man and wife; perhaps they are only two elderly persons once in love with one another during their younger years. It does not matter. The significance of the poem rests upon the realization, expressed by one of the two, that there comes a time in the Indian summer of life, after all aspects of the sentimental, blooming love of physical beauty and strong emotions are faded and any reminders of it gone, when a man and woman may find richness of contact and association through a sharing of intellectual thoughts and feelings, can 'descant' upon topics which, in their very impersonal character, can yet bring two such persons closer together and compensate for the loss of the more youthful phases of love.

"Not only is the thought expressed unique and even, in its scope and implications, profound, but the conciseness and vividness ·with which it is expressed are admirable. The very first line, every important word arrestingly emphasized, 'sets the stage,' as it were, for the thought to follow. The resort to the things of the mind and intellectual experience are to be contrasted with the long interim of silence between the two as long as neither was able to transcend the restrictions and limitations of pure emotional attachment, when words were inade-

167

quate vessels for the transfer of sentiment. All other lovers are estranged (because they could never find satisfaction in the mode of intimacy and contact which these lovers have) or are dead, so that all reminders of the first flush of youthful love are gone. The image of lamplight 'hid under its shade' is striking, a lamplight which is 'unfriendly,' since it would serve only to show up the transience of the physical beauty or attractiveness of the couple; yet the atmosphere of intimacy between the two is emphasized in the very next line, with subtle reference to the 'unfriendly night shut out.' 'Bodily decrepitude is wisdom,' for young love did not recognize the value and power of such exchange of thoughts and association as this couple can.

"The tone is not that of grief, although a hint of sadness is suggested, a sadness at this very transience of youthful love. But essentially the tone is that of resignation and acceptance, of this phase of 'love' which compensates for its previous immature counterpart. And this tone is consistent and splendidly suggested throughout."

16. For the complexity of the influences on criticism and the richness of the criticism itself, see Morton Dauwen Zabel's *Literary opinion in America* (Harper, 1937), a brilliant analysis with important texts. For another interpretation of the contemporary critical renaissance, see Alfred Kazin's *On native grounds* (Reynal and Hitchcock, 1942), pp. 400-52.

17. Ransom's critical position is stated most fully in the essay, "Wanted: An Ontological Critic," in his *The new criticism* (New Directions, 1941). The pioneer textbook incorporating the Richards-Ransom influence was *Understanding poetry*, by Cleanth Brooks and Robert Penn Warren (Henry Holt and Company, 1938). Other textbooks with similar objectives, if with somewhat different techniques, are *Reading poems* (Oxford University Press, 1941) by Wright Thomas and S. G. Brown, and *The art of reading poetry* (Farrar and Rinehart, 1941), by Earl Daniels.

18. R. M. Hutchins, *The higher learning in America* (Yale University Press, 1936), pp. 78-79. Dean T. H-E. Chen outlines the development of the "great books" idea thus: "Selection and compilation of the books began as early as the time of the World War, when John Erskine and his associates undertook to construct a curriculum for the American Expeditionary Force University in Beaune at the end of the War. The early return of the Expeditionary Force precluded the opportunity of using the list of books which had been selected, but when Erskine went to Columbia he brought the list with him, and there it was adopted for use in connection with honors courses. At the same time Scott Buchanan made use of such a list with adult reading courses in connection with the People's Institute and the New York Public Libraries. Buchanan later went to the University of Virginia, where he worked further on the project with Stringfellow Barr, while his associates at the People's Institute carried the idea to the University of Chicago." Chen, *op. cit.*, p. 70. Dean Chen does not mention the brief period of Buchanan's and Barr's appointments at the University of Chicago (1936-37), during which they devoted themselves almost exclusively to thinking out the problem of the place of the humanities in the liberal arts curriculum.

168

19. President Hutchins regards the study of great books as the basis of general education. "We have then for general education a course of study consisting of the greatest books of the western world and the arts of reading, writing, thinking, and speaking, together with mathematics, the best exemplar of the processes of human reason. If our hope has been to frame a curriculum which educes the elements of our common human nature, this program should realize our hope. If we wish to prepare the young for intelligent action, this course of study should assist us; for they will have learned what has been done in the past, and what the greatest men have thought. They will have learned how to think themselves. If we wish to lay a basis for advanced study, that basis is provided. If we wish to secure true universities, we may look forward to them, because students and professors may acquire through this course of study a common stock of ideas and common methods of dealing with them. *All the needs of general education in America seem to be satisfied by this curriculum.*" Quoted in R. Freeman Butts, *op. cit.*, pp. 292-93.

20. The most overt result of President Hutchins' theory has been the creation at St. John's College at Annapolis of a curriculum that consists almost exclusively of a study of the hundred best books. The creation of this curriculum was the work of President Hutchins' friends and associates, Scott Buchanan and Stringfellow Barr. For some account of this curriculum, its philosophy, and its operation, see T. H-E. Chen, *op. cit.*, pp. 66-76.

21. *Requirements for degrees in English* (University of Chicago, second edition, October, 1939), introductory, pp. iii-v. "The objectives here defined are achieved by means of courses in the history of English and American literature, in language, and in criticism and the analysis of ideas. An important feature of the plan, however, involves the student's private preparation for examinations on a sizable list of 'set books,' ranging from Aristotle's *Poetics* to the essays of T. S. Eliot, and including poems, plays, novels, and expository and argumentative writing. The extent to which these objectives have been achieved is determined by the student's performance in an extensive series of elaborate examinations:"

(1) Literary history—a three-hour examination, mainly objective in character, on the history of English and American literature;

(2) Criticism (three hours): "The subject matter of this part of the examination is an artistic work (play, novel, or group of poems) set for independent study at least three months before the examination . . . The questions making up the examination . . . call for two kinds of equipment: on the one hand, a clear understanding of the major terms, distinctions, and methods involved in the various modes of critical analysis and judgment, as embodied in the treatises of such critics as Aristotle, Horace, Longinus, Sidney, Dryden, Johnson, Coleridge, Arnold, and Eliot; on the other hand, an ability to apply the principles appropriate to the chief modes of criticism sensitively and clearly in the discussion of particular works." *Ibid.*, p. 4.

(3) Analysis of ideas (three hours): "The texts constituting the sub-

169

ject matter of the examination are works the specific end of which is the exposition of ideas or the persuasion of an audience to some particular belief: the questions, consequently, have to do with such matters as the purpose of the work or the problem with which it deals, the meaning of its terms and distinctions, the order of its parts, the content of its arguments and their relation to each other, the appropriateness of its style, and the like." *Ibid.*, p. 5.

(4) Masterpieces—two three-hour examinations: These examinations are intended to demonstrate "detailed knowledge of the works to which the questions relate and some skill in applying the techniques of esthetic or of intellectual analysis in well-expressed and well-ordered discussions; the examination, in other words, is designed primarily to find out, not whether the books have been read, but how well they have been understood." *Ibid.*, p. 3. It will be observed that in the program for the bachelor's degree in English at Chicago the disciplines of history and of linguistics play little or no part. Training in these disciplines is deferred until the student is preparing for his candidacy for the master's or the doctor's degree.

For a statement of the critical position of the Chicago group, see "Two Essays in Practical Criticism: Prefatory Note" (R. S. Crane); "An Analysis of a Lyric Poem" (Norman F. Maclean); "Sailing to Byzantium" (Elder Olson); *The University* [of Kansas City] *Review*, Vol. 8, No. 3, pp. 199-219. For a critique of the theoretical assumptions of the Chicago group, see Kenneth Burke, "The Problem of the Intrinsic," *Accent*, Winter, 1943, pp. 80-94.

22. It may be of interest to quote a briefer attempt to outline the influences that lie behind the contemporary movement back to the text. "In recent years a healthy reaction has taken place which recognizes that the study of literature should, first and foremost, concentrate on the actual works of art themselves. The old methods of classical rhetoric, poetics, or metrics are found insufficient and must be replaced or at least supplemented by new methods based on a survey of the wider range of forms in modern literature. In France the method of *explication de textes*, in Germany the formal analyses based on parallels with the history of fine arts, cultivated by Oscar Walzel, and especially the brilliant movement of the Russian formalists and their Czech and Polish followers have brought new stimuli to the study of the literary work which we are only beginning to see properly and to analyze adequately. In England some of the followers of I. A. Richards have paid close attention to the text of poetry and also in this country a group of critics have made a study of the work of art the center of their interest. All these recent studies have one common characteristic: they try to bridge the dangerous gulf between content and form and to overcome the isolation of individual features like meter and diction; they attempt to analyze the work of art without ignoring its unity and integrity. Among these methods, those devised by the Russian formalists seem to me most valuable, especially with the modifications of the theory propounded by the Prague Linguistic Circle. They introduce the concept of 'structure' which includes both content and form as far as they are organized

for esthetic purposes. The work of art is considered as a whole dynamic system of signs serving a specific esthetic purpose." Wellek, *op. cit.*, pp. 97-98.

CHAPTER IV

1. "A survey of 35 lesser institutions found, for example, that only 32 per cent of all staff members made any contribution to printed literature over a five-year period and that the median number of contributions was only 1.3 items. An inquiry conducted by the American Historical Association in various types of colleges and universities revealed that only 25 per cent of doctors of philosophy in history are consistent producers. Similarly, 'among 1,888 persons in the United States who took the Ph.D. in mathematics between 1862 and 1933, after graduation 46 per cent prepared no published papers; 19 per cent only 1 paper; 8 per cent only 2 papers; 11 per cent 3 to 5 papers; 6 per cent 6 to 10 papers; 2 per cent 21 to 30 papers; and 2 per cent more than 30 papers.' These figures indicate that if the average academician in the typical college or university depended on his quantitative scholarly output for employee advancement, in rank and status, the hierarchical pyramid would show very few members at or near the top. The actual situation in such institutions proves, therefore, that the research function is not participated in extensively by most faculty members—a partial corollary of its being considered less essential than teaching and other kinds of performance appraised by the administration." Wilson, *op. cit.*, pp. 107-08.

2. Professor W. W. Charters, in reviewing Wilson's book, suggests the need for stressing the satisfactions rather than the dissatisfactions, the easeful as well as the stressful periods, in the academic existence. He objects to the formula that underlies *The academic man.* "The formula is to locate the stresses, strains, sore spots, and problems of the profession . . . Our quarrel with the formula of stresses as the basis for the analysis of a profession rests upon the assumption that it is not the sole basis of analysis . . . A complementary formula must be used to give the proper balance—the formula of satisfactions. Many professors find satisfaction in the enthusiastic teaching of groups of young people who, when all aspersions have been weighed, are the cream of their generation of high-school graduates. No stress formula discovers this. Professors find enjoyment in the flexibility in their schedules: they work their fifty-five hours a week but when they like—in the daytime, at night, over week ends. They do not punch a time clock in fact or in spirit. Many professors feel that nowhere is there such an opportunity as in the graduate school to get the thrill of training young expert specialists, watch them grow under intelligent tuition. University people enjoy the feeling of relative security in comparison with industry and commerce so that while wages are not extravagant, the position is secure." By permission of the author and *The Journal of Higher Education*, November, 1942, pp. 454-55.

3. "Some of the qualities that are alleged to characterize a superior teacher are attractiveness of personality, the power of clear exposition,

breadth of knowledge, ability to stimulate student curiosity, sympathy with student interests, enthusiasm for learning, and an accurate sense of values, a sense of humor, sincerity, and good taste in personal relations. Other traits would be added to this list in any extensive inventory." Haggerty, *op. cit.*, p. 228.

4. "During the 1941-42 academic year, 3,243 doctoral dissertations were accepted by American and Canadian universities. . . . For the first time in many years, the University of Chicago *nosed out* Columbia University in the number of degrees granted. The number of doctorates has been increasing steadily, reaching an all-time high of 3,526 theses in 1941. The current year is the first to show a decrease. Chicago, usually second, leads with 197 degrees, and Columbia, usually first, is next with 187. The University of Wisconsin ranks third, its usual position, with 163 . . . As for many years, chemistry leads all subjects with 588 dissertations. Education, with 344, is second; economics, with 181, is third. The following are represented by 100 or more: English, physics, modern history, biochemistry, psychology, botany, religion and zoology. Three fields of study are about equal in popularity: physical sciences with 873; social sciences, with 858; and biological sciences, with 847 dissertations. The humanities were represented by 403. . . . The largest number granted in a single field by one institution was 52 in *education* by New York University and the same number in religion by the Catholic University of America." New York *Times*, December 13, 1942, p. E 7. The statistics in the article quoted are taken from E. A. Henry's *Doctoral dissertations accepted by American universities,* No. 9, 1941-42. The italics within the quotation are mine.

5. "The stillbirth malady affecting so many Ph.D.'s is common knowledge and a source of great concern to graduate schools that have not yet learned to prevent its occurrence. It appears sometimes as if the feeble stream of intellectual vitality had been wholly exhausted in the effort to obtain a degree. When that happens, the degree is not a symbol of continuous and vigorous mental life; it merely marks the place where that life dried up and to a great extent ceased." Haggerty, *op. cit.*, Vol. II, "The Faculty," p. 95.

6. "It is a curious abnormality of some college instructors that they hold in contempt all discussion of teaching methods. Probably in no other profession could one discover the same indifference to information and considered treatment of the problems that constitute the core of the individual's chief activity. The charge that published discussions are superficial and inadequate lessens not a whit the significance of instructional problems or the need for sound discussion of them. If available literature is as inadequate and superficial as it is sometimes claimed to be, the only intelligent response of critics is the production of a better treatment of the subject. Of course, the charge of puerility against existing literature and the current treatment of instructional problems is chiefly a mechanism of defense to justify a lack of interest and the absence of desire to improve one's work." Haggerty, *op. cit.*, Vol. III, "The Educational Problem," p. 277.

CHAPTER V

1. "All the achievements of man, which together constitute civilization, represent two things. On the one hand, they represent the nature of the world which made them possible. But on the other hand, they represent no less the human will-to-values which demanded them. Thus the knowledge possessed by man represents indeed facts which were there to be known, but it also represents, and just as truly, the interests which caused man to notice some facts and neglect others, to ask this question rather than that, to seek the explanations that he desired but did not at first perceive. The tool and other material artifacts of man represent properties which the substance employed possessed, but they equally represent human ends, the means to which he wanted to command. Similarly, the social institutions that man has brought into being represent capacities of behavior possessed by those who live under them; but they no less represent modes of living that once did not exist, but which man desired to establish. And the works of art that he has created represent qualities which belonged to the materials used and forms which they were capable of assuming, but they represent fully as much feelings and ideas that man wanted to express, and experiences of soul and mind that he wished to be able to reproduce at will.

"It is, then, of the essence of knowledge, to constitute man's answer to man's question; of the essence of instruments, to constitute nature's means to man's ends; of the essence of works of art, to constitute the embodiment in nature of man's emotional and intellectual intent. Schopenhauer believed the active essence of man to be the will-to-live, and Nietzsche declared it to be the will-to-power; but both of these characterizations are too narrow. The active essence of man is rather the will-to-values, and the whole of the civilization that man has created constitutes in its various aspects an objectification of his will to manifold values, no less than an exhibition of the nature and potentialities of the world which confronted that will." C. J. Ducasse, "The Relation of Philosophy to General Education" (Unpublished manuscript), pp. 48-49.

2. This classification—the one in vogue at the University of Chicago —is repeated with slight variations in a considerable number of contemporary colleges and universities. Obviously, the classification becomes increasingly difficult as subjects and departments multiply. In the liberal arts college, the classification is likely to give rise to no special problem of alignment. Certain subjects, however, offer special problems of affiliation. Biochemistry, for instance, is obviously an attempt to link one of the physical and one of the biological sciences. Since, as I judge, the bio-chemist puts the emphasis on the bio rather than on the chemistry, his affiliation is almost bound to be with the biological sciences. Psychology also constitutes a problem in classification. The decision in this matter is likely to be made on the basis of the particular interests of the individual or departments involved. The social psychologist obviously feels closest to the social sciences; the physiological psychologist, who seems to be pre-empting the field, is right in claiming his place among the biological scientists. The history

of psychology—and, I am inclined to say, its decline and fall—might be traced from its separation from philosophy, through its flirtation with the social sciences, to its alliance with biology. A more difficult and consequential problem is raised by history. When the divisional organization was introduced at Chicago, the Department of History was of two minds about its proper classification. Finally, those who viewed history primarily as a science were allowed to affiliate themselves with the Division of the Social Sciences and those who considered history primarily as one of the arts—or at least as a science with the closest ties with the humanities—were allowed to join the Division of the Humanities. The complexity of the problems involving the humanities is suggested by the fact that at Chicago nineteen departments belong to the Humanities Division: Art, Comparative Religion, English, German, Greek, History, Latin, Linguistics, Music, New Testament and Early Christian Literature, Oriental Languages and Literatures (i.e., Oriental History, Archeology, Hebrew and Old Testament, Aramaic, and Akkadian), Philosophy, Romance Languages and Literatures (i.e., French, Spanish, Italian, and Portuguese). The problem of arriving at common objectives for this conglomeration of studies and special interests is a tremendously difficult one.

3. "We may, if we like (says a recent writer), think of all knowledge as assuming the form of a triangle, of which one apex is occupied by the natural and physical sciences, another by the social sciences and the third by the humanities. The natural and physical sciences deal with man's environment, the most remote as well as the most immediate; the social sciences with man in his associations with other men; while the humanities concern themselves with the manifestations of his spiritual existence. [Waldo G. Leland, "Recent Trends in the Humanities," *Science*, N.S., Vol. LXXIX, p. 281.]" Quoted in R. B. Perry, "A Definition of the Humanities," in *The meaning of the humanities* (Princeton University Press, 1938), p. 31.

4. "The natural sciences have in common an interest in the world of 'fact' as contrasted with the realm of 'values.' This distinction between 'fact' and 'value' does not deny the reality or objectivity of values; it merely marks the well-recognized difference between value and non-value situations. The pure sciences are descriptive and explanatory rather than evaluative; their interpretations are concerned with the structure and behavior of natural phenomena rather than with their significance for man. Relying upon a distinctive type of observation, experimentation, and interpretation, they attempt to lay bare the regularities and irregularities which characterize events in space and time. No matter what he is studying, the scientist maintains his objective and external approach, and he applies his criteria of scientific judgment in all cases alike. Students of the arts and literatures, morality and religion, in contrast, must enter sympathetically into value experiences and attempt to set up standards of appraisal." Greene, *et al.*, *op. cit.*, pp. 49-50.

5. The objectives of the physical science course at Colgate University are stated thus: "To provide the student with a fair panoramic view of the universe in which he lives and his relation to it . . . What the student is expected to get from the course is a definite concept of the

174

physical world, an appreciation of the scientific method and its role in the intellectual life of the race, and an understanding of the contributions of the physical sciences to the solution of some of our contemporary problems." Some of the topics discussed in the course are the solar system, the history and age of the earth, matter and energy, the atomic theory, and spectroscopy. Quoted from a folder describing the text, *Atoms, rocks, and galaxies, a survey in physical science*, J. S. Allen *et al.* (Harper, 1938).

6. These phrases are quoted from a folder describing the purposes and content of the textbook, *The human organism and the world of life, a survey in biological science*, by Clarence W. Young *et al.* (Harper, 1938), prepared by a group of the faculty at Colgate University. The objectives of the survey course in the Biological Sciences at the University of Chicago are indicated thus: "(1) to cultivate such skills and habits of scientific thinking as are exemplified in biology; (2) to describe and interpret the machinery of the organic world and the major concepts of biology; and (3) to provide practical information about biology desirable for a citizen in the modern world." "The College and the Divisions for the Sessions of 1943-44" (The University of Chicago Press, 1943), p. 54.

7. "Many phenomena—meteorological, biological, medical, social, economic—are too complicated for adequate analysis, and are not observable under sufficiently varied or controlled conditions for the reliable application of these methods (the simple inductive method and the deductive-inductive method) . . . The Statistical Method is an attempt to deal with such complex and exceptionally difficult phenomena in a scientific manner . . . Like other scientific methods statistical method aims at the discovery of connections between natural phenomena. And it does so by a close study of their concurrences or sequences. Unlike the so-called method of simple enumeration, it notes and records carefully not only actual occurrences and sequences, but also exceptions; it makes observations over as large and varied a field as possible; and cautiously draws conclusions that will fit all the observed facts. The observation of only a few cases of concurrence, or sequence, or concomitant variation, among certain phenomena, especially when the conditions are not under control and the full circumstances are not known, makes it impossible to distinguish a causal connection between the phenomena from a casual coincidence between them. But the observation of a large number of cases over a wide and varied range of circumstances, an exact record of positive and negative cases, and of variations between series of instances, may justify a highly probable conclusion about a causal connection between the phenomena concerned . . . The important thing to bear in mind is that no amount of statistical technique can serve as an adequate substitute for a direct knowledge of, and familiarity with, the phenomena under investigation." Abraham Wolf, "Scientific Method," *Encyclopædia Britannica*, Fourteenth Edition, 1929, Vol. XX, pp. 131-32.

Whether the statistical method can properly be applied to determining the factors that make for a happy marriage—a problem of a highly subjective nature—may very well be questioned! The statistical study made in behalf of Stephens College under the direction of W. W. Charters to determine the activities of women in present-day society seems to furnish a striking example of a dependence on the statistical method where a little common sense would have saved some foundation a great deal of money. "Three hundred women in thirty-seven states were asked to keep diaries of their activities, problems, and thoughts over a period of time in accordance with specific directions . . . The diaries contained 7,500 items 'which included all the activities of home makers and all the activities of professional women which they carried on outside their regular vocations.' These were, upon analysis, classified under twenty-four categories. Further analysis revealed seven areas of activities which were found to be common to all women, irrespective of vocation . . . (1) communication, oral and written; (2) physical health; (3) mental health; (4) civic relations: social, economic, and political problems; (5) esthetic appreciation; (6) morals, religion, and a philosophy; and (7) consumption." T. H-E. Chen, *Developing patterns of the college curriculum in the United States,* "Southern California Education Monographs," No. 10 (University of Southern California Press, 1940), pp. 106-07. Surely this is an instance of a statistical mountain bringing forth a common-sensical mouse!

8. Quoted from a folder describing the text *Men, groups, and the community,* a survey in the social sciences, by T. H. Robinson *et al.* (Harper, 1939). This particular text and the course in which it is used explain "the important features of the community, such as the specialization of activities, folk-ways, mores, institutions, laws, culture, and communication; . . . certain features of community life, such as supplies of goods and services, family relations, the adjustment of young people to the life of the community, the educational system, the characteristics of representative government, and public service; . . . the nature of social stability and social change"; . . . "private and public ways of improving our social organization and solving our social problems in the various fields."

9. "The humanities, unlike the sciences, are primarily concerned with values and critical appraisal. Since their subject matter is man's experiences of value and his ideals and standards, they are directed to what is most intimately and peculiarly human. The disciplines usually entitled the 'humanities' concern themselves with the apprehension, analysis, and interpretation of expressed insights in the realms of morality, religion, art, and literature. In so far as history and philosophy concern themselves with these insights, they too must be included among the humanistic disciplines." Greene, *et al., op. cit.,* p. 57.

10. The philosopher Max Otto has said, "The vast economic, material body of the world lacks a mind to match it, and is not animated by a commensurate moral spirit. This backwardness is the tragic inadequacy of our time. It is the problem which, more than any other, calls upon philosophy for new vision and creativeness." Quoted in *Time,* December 14, 1942, p. 124, in its review of Charles A. Beard and Mary R. Beard's *The American spirit* (Macmillan, 1942).

11. "Abraham Flexner, in his Taylorian Lecture at Oxford in 1928, stated 'if science and industry are held down to their essential part, it

becomes clear that somewhere a rational system of values must be developed, outside science as such, outside industry as such, and yet ultimately operative within both. It is this sense of value that will make distinctions and thus determine the direction of human development. The assessment of values, in so far as human beings are affected, constitutes the unique burden of humanism.' [Abraham Flexner, *The burden of humanism,* p. 35.]" Patricia Beesley, *The revival of the humanities in American education* (Columbia University Press, 1940), p. 53.

12. "Under 'Humanism' I include what conforms to the standards of value in domains such as those of Literature, of Music, of Art, and of Religion. The standards we employ in these domains stand in some contrast with other standards by which we test values in science and in metaphysics. They imply on their faces reference to self-conscious personality, and they are less abstract." Viscount Haldane, *The philosophy of humanism and of other subjects* (London: John Murray, 1922), p. 35.

13. "Of the more humane disciplines, history is closest to the sciences in its objective, descriptive temper and its close attention to details, which it seeks to understand rather than to modify in any practical way. Philosophy shares the objectivity of the historical temper, and its theoretic rather than practical attitude. But its range is far wider and its conclusions more generalized. History concerns itself with the pageant of human life in the time order. Philosophy takes account also of physical nature in its microscopic and macrocosmic aspects; scrutinizes the principles of logical method, of experience and knowledge, of existence and value; and continually tries to bring its conceptual lenses to focus upon ultimate reality, the Absolute, or God. It knows nothing in so detailed a way as the competent historian knows his chosen period. It tries to see everything in terms of its essential nature, with eternity or cosmic time ('real duration'), not earthly clock-and-calendar time, as its frame.

"Literature and the fine arts, like history, focus their attention upon concrete details; even more minutely, indeed, and with more ingenious camera angles, than sober history itself may countenance. Like philosophy, however, they range through physical nature and the regions of abstract form, as well as up and down the panorama of human life. They seek to elicit from details, shrewdly chosen and artfully illuminated, something of universal human significance. Their media of expression are far more varied than those available for history and philosophy, even when graphic devices, the cinema and sound track, and the dramatic pageant are included among the vehicles of modern historical writing. And more than either history or philosophy, literature and the fine arts enlist the full personal being of the composer, and seek to move the feelings no less than the thoughts of the observer. They have rightfully a degree of subjectivity and persuasiveness which good history and philosophy must take pains to avoid.

"Theology stands, in a manner, between these two pairs of disciplines: closer in its procedures to history and philosophy, closer in its intent to literature and the fine arts, and more than any of them directly seeking to move men's wills. Such is its horizontal range." R. L.

Calhoun, "Theology and the Humanities," in *The meaning of the humanities* (Princeton University Press, 1938), pp. 130-31.

14. "The content of literature and of the arts is intrinsically humane. It presents life concretely, presenting models for admiration or condemnation—for imitation or rejection. It enlarges the range of immediate experience, and communicates it feelingly; it stimulates the imagination and breaks the molds of habit; it expresses the diverse visions and aspirations of great men; it integrates the different cultural elements of a society or an epoch; it embodies beauty and commends it as an object of disinterested pleasure; at its best, it brings a sense of moral elevation." Perry, *op. cit.*, p. 39.

15. "The artist's approach to reality, unlike that of the scientist, is essentially evaluative. He is always concerned with the significance of his subject matter for man and with the meaning of human experience. His approach to reality is never cold, impersonal, and dispassionate. Art, at its best, exhibits unusual sympathetic insight. The artist is distinguished from other men by his pre-eminent ability to discern, with imaginative power, what the average man apprehends only feebly and confusedly. The arts are therefore the most effective language at man's disposal for the apprehension and communication of whatever endows human experience with significance." Greene, *et al., op. cit.*, pp. 61-62.

16. "The place of philosophy in a liberal arts college will depend upon the extent to which other subjects realize or renounce their humanistic possibilities. If the natural sciences confine themselves to technique and technology, then it will fall to philosophy to delineate the spectacle of nature in a course on 'cosmology'; and to present the scientific spirit of man in a course on 'the philosophy of science.' If the social sciences yield their autonomy and become a province of natural science, then the meaning of society and the purposes of human institutions will be left to a course on ethics, theory of value or social philosophy. If history ceases to reconstruct and interpret the life of man, then that task will fall to a philosophy of history. If literature and the fine arts are superseded by their accessories and adjuncts, the history of philosophy, or esthetics, or a philosophy of criticism will become the sole exponent of the intuitions and values of which literature and the fine arts are the vehicle." Perry, *op. cit.*, pp. 40-41.

17. Ducasse, *op. cit.*, pp. 76-77. While maintaining that philosophy ought to be given a position of prime importance in the hierarchy of humanistic studies, one is forced reluctantly to acknowledge that many philosophers are unequal to the responsibility thus imposed upon them. Their inadequacy is due, not merely to the limitations *per se* of human nature but to the fact that graduate training in philosophy and research in it suffer from the same blight of "specialism" and "scientism" which has been one of the major causes of the decline in the repute and importance of the humanities.

18. "It seems anomalous that, of the hundreds of surveys of institutions of higher learning, in less than one-tenth was any effort made at systematic classroom visiting reported. In less than half of this tenth was the visit more than incidental. Of course, classroom visiting, which immediately tends to produce artificial conditions, is likely to be keenly

resented by many college and university instructors. . . . Even the extensive survey whose sole object was college and university teaching . . . so recently conducted by the American Association of University Professors, contains no evidence that the committee or the field director actually observed directly any college or university teaching in any of the nearly one hundred institutions visited. *The traditional sanctity of the university classroom was not violated.* The survey of higher education in Maine . . . conducted under the direction of the largest teachers college in America, contains an entire chapter of almost 50 pages written by 'a specialist in the study of problems of instruction,' but it is based entirely upon indirect evidence and contains no suggestion that the writer stepped into a single college classroom in any of the three institutions studied." W. C. Eells, *Surveys of American higher education* (The Carnegie Foundation for the Advancement of Teaching, 1937), pp. 117-18. Italics mine.